INSIGHT P

CW00369500

SYD

APA PUBLICATIONS
Part of the Langenscheidt Publishing Group
L

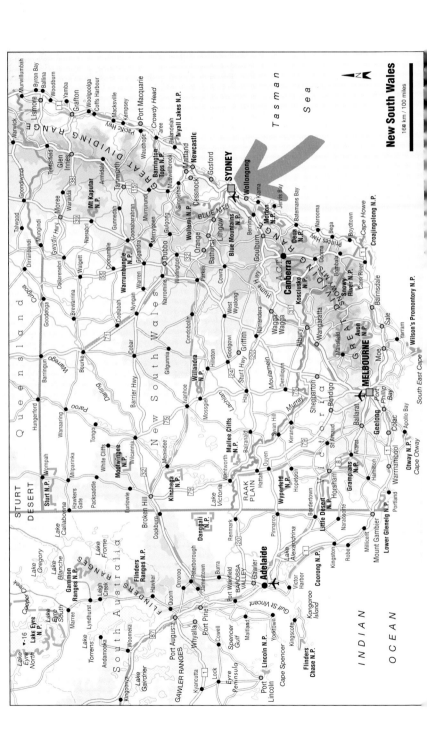

New South Wales

160 km / 100 miles

Welcome

This guidebook combines the interests and enthusiasms of two of the world's best-known information providers: Insight Guides, who have set the standard for visual travel guides since 1970, and Discovery Channel, the world's premier source of non-fiction television programming. Its aim is to show visitors the best of Sydney and its surroundings in a series of tailor-made itineraries. An exciting metropolis famed for its harbour and dramatic Opera House, a melting pot of Asian, Oceanian, European and American cultures, and the venue for the 2000 Olympic Games, the city is packed with attractions.

The task of devising the itineraries was split between two Sydney-based travel writers and photographers, David McGonigal and John Borthwick. Their brief was to link the city's essential sights, but also to include some of its more off-beat corners that only inhabitants of Sydney are likely to know. This edition of the guide was updated and expanded by Ingrid Ohlsson, Insight's correspondent in Sydney.

Supporting the itineraries are sections on history and culture, shopping, eating out, nightlife and festivals, plus a detailed practical information section covering everything from money matters to getting around, and including a list of hand-picked hotels.

David McGonigal left Australia in 1976 but returned to Sydney four years later to make it his permanent home. His love affair with this warm and wonderful harbourside city endures to this day. 'Few would contest Sydney's claim to be one of the world's most scenically spectacular cities, a shimmering delight of sunlight off water and golden beaches', he says. This Sydneysider's unabashed affection for the city is obvious in the itineraries he has put together.

John Borthwick had heaps of fun researching and writing this book. In doing so he rediscovered the city or, as he puts it, he 'became a tourist at home'. Borthwick recognises that much has been made of Sydney being 'the best address on earth'. For him, this simply translates to being at home.

EXCURSIONS

These four excursions are ideal for those who wish to experience some of the raw, natural beauty for which Australia is famous.

LEISURE ACTIVITIES

CALENDAR OF EVENTS

PRACTICAL INFORMATION

MAPS

INDEX AND CREDITS

◄Preceding Pages: Sydney Opera House
◄Following Pages: Bondi Beach from the Pavilion

History & Culture

Nearly 50,000 years ago, when the first Aborigines reached the site of what was to become Sydney, they found a long, dry valley about 10km (6 miles) inland from the sea. Some 10,000 years ago, melting ice-caps raised the sea level, flooding the valley to form what was to become Sydney Harbour, and bringing the coastline to the sands of today's famous Bondi and Manly beaches.

An estimated 3,000 Aborigines, divided into three tribes or language groups, were living in the Sydney region when the first Europeans arrived. About 1,500 Eora people roamed the harbour foreshores, sheltering in caves, hunting possums, wallabies, snakes and other wild animals, and gathering shellfish and bush food. The Duruk people lived to the north of the harbour and the Tharawal to the south. Aboriginal society developed intricate social structures and complex religious beliefs based on an intense spiritual identification with the land. The only Aboriginal artefacts that have survived consist of a few Stone-Age tools and some rock art, most notably carvings depicting the ancestral spirits of the Kurringgai people, who lived in what is now in Ku-ring-gai Chase National Park on Sydney's northern fringes.

European Discovery

On 29 April 1770 Captain James Cook sailed the *Endeavour* into a sheltered bay where he noted a 'fine meadow'. The north, south and west coasts of the continent had already been explored by Dutch, Portuguese and Spanish navigators over the previous two centuries. None had ventured as far as the east coast, which Captain Cook followed from approximately the present border between New South Wales and Victoria, through Botany Bay (south of today's Sydney) to the tip of Queensland at Cape York. The *Endeavour* spent a week in Botany Bay but the crew had little contact with its 3,000 Aborigines. Cook noted that 'all they seemed to want was for us to be gone.'

At first, the British government was slow to realise the potential of the land which Cook claimed in the name of the crown. However, the American Declaration of Independence in 1776 brought an abrupt end to Britain's practice of transporting convicts to America's southern plantations and penal settlements such as Georgia. British prisons subsequently filled up and the rotting hulks of ships on the Thames took the overflow. In August 1786, Lord Sydney (Thomas Townsend), the British home secretary, instructed the admiralty to send a naval fleet filled with convicts to Botany Bay. This marked the inauspicious birth of a new nation.

.eft: an early inhabitant
Right: Captain Cook

First Settlement

On 13 May 1787, a fleet of 11 ships set sail from Portsmouth; it reached Botany Bay, 22,500 km (14,000 miles) away, on 20 January 1788. Finding the bay's water supplies inadequate, Captain Arthur Phillip moved on to Port Jackson (merely noted by Cook in passing), which he called 'the finest harbour in the world'. The whole colony moved to what Phillip named 'Sydney Cove'. On 26 January 1788, the Union Jack was raised for the first time over the settlement of 568 male and 191 female convicts, and 200 marines accompanied by 27 wives and 25 children. In its first two years, some 50 percent of the colony's Aborigines were killed by smallpox; after 50 years of white settlement, fewer than 300 Aborigines remained in the region. But many of Sydney's suburbs were given Aboriginal names.

The spectre of starvation haunted the settlements' first few years. The few Aboriginees who did not succumb to smallpox prudently kept their distance, leaving the settlers to begin the long struggle of learning how to survive in this strange, unpredictable land. By mid-1790, the entire colony, now known as 'New South Wales', would have died from starvation were it not for the timely arrival of a supply ship. Not long afterwards, the Second Fleet sailed into port in a terrible condition: 267 convicts had died on the long sea voyage and a further 124 died soon after their arrival. The settlers clung to the foreshores of Sydney Cove for a considerable time. Captain Phillip, now the governor, devised a coherent town plan but it never got off the drawing board and, as a result, Sydney's street grid remains haphazard to this day. Phillip was followed by governors Hunter, King and then the infamous Bligh. The latter came to Sydney on his first appointment after the famed mutiny on the *Bounty*.

Beginnings of Nationhood

The historic 12-year term of Governor Lachlan Macquarie (1810–21) saw New South Wales evolve from foundling colonial settlement to fledgling community. Sydney continues to bear the stamp of Macquarie and his principal architect, the forger, convict and genius Francis Greenway. Macquarie established a designated street width (with footpaths); Greenway designed churches, including St James' in the city, St Matthew's at Windsor and St Luke's in Liverpool, that still attract numerous visitors today. Macquarie gave Greenway a pardon after he designed Hyde Park Barracks (still standing in Macquarie Street), but the architect's fortunes suffered a steep decline after the departure of his patron; Commissioner Bigge considered Greenway's work to be 'too grand for an infant colony'. In 1817 Macquarie became the first official to use the word 'Australia' in correspondence. The colonialist Sir George Shaw coined the term in 1794 from the Greek *terra australis* (south land). Mathew Flinders used it in his *Voyage to Terra Australis* in 1814.

The population of Sydney increased rapidly as free settlers joined the con-

Above: plaque marking Cook's arrival. **Above right**: Aborigines in Sydney's new streets in the 18th century. **Right**: the city in the mid-19th century

victs. This population explosion was remarkable considering that it took 24 years to find a way across the Blue Mountains to the pasture lands of the west. Still, by 1820, the town of Sydney barely covered 2 sq km (1 sq mile). The country's first street, George Street, evolved from a bullock track, and the first road leading out of Sydney was built to Parramatta in 1794.

Convict migration to New South Wales only came to an end in 1840, by which time a total of some 83,000 prisoners had been sent there for their crimes. Most, making a virtue out of necessity, stayed on to make a new home in the colony. (It's worth recalling the remarks of Charles Darwin, who visited Sydney in 1836. Darwin concluded that 'as a real system of reform it has failed… but as a means of making men outwardly honest – of converting vagabonds most useless in one hemisphere into active citizens of another, and thus giving birth to a new and splendid country – a grand centre of civilisation – it has succeeded to a degree perhaps unparalleled in history'.)

Gold Rush

The town of Sydney was declared a city in 1842. Within a decade, E.H. Hargraves made history on becoming the first person in the country to discover gold, near Bathurst, on the other side of the Blue Mountains. Hargraves had returned from the California gold fields claiming that they reminded him

of parts of New South Wales. Turning a deaf ear to a general chorus of ridicule, he proceeded from Sydney to Bathurst with an acquaintance; before long he announced that they were standing on gold. His first panful of dirt did indeed produce the precious metal and he famously declared: 'Here it is. This is a memorable day in the history of New South Wales. I shall be a baronet, and you will be knighted, and my old horse will be stuffed, put in a glass case and sent to the British Museum!' Unfortunately Hargraves' optimistic prophesying was less successful than his gold prospecting. The rest of his life was uneventful and he died in 1891.

Hargraves' discovery marked the beginning of a rush that proved to be an enormous boon to Sydney's fortunes: the city's population skyrocketed from 54,000 in 1851 to 96,000 in 1861. The infrastructure had to be completely revamped to meet the demands of the influx. By 1885, the main city streets were paved with wooden blocks, thus finally removing the dust pall which had plagued Sydney for years. Buildings befitting a city belonging to Britain were constructed towards the end of Queen Victoria's lengthy reign. These included the town hall in 1889, the Customs House in 1885 and the Art Gallery. In 1895 the American writer Mark Twain visited Sydney and declared it to be 'an English city with American trimmings'. The same accusation is frequently made today.

Australian Federation

On 1 January 1901 the Commonwealth of Australia came into existence. Thousands of Sydney's inhabitants poured into Centennial Park to witness the swearing-in of Australia's first governor-general. Sydney, a vibrant city with established literary and arts movements, had come of age. But it was also trying desperately to recover from the economic depression of 1892. To a great extent, the Australian colonies traded themselves out of trouble by considerably expanding the areas under wheat cultivation. In 1900 the city suffered a more immediate urban problem: an outbreak of bubonic plague

was responsible for the deaths of 112 people. The silver lining of this particular cloud became apparent in the following years when the slums in The Rocks area were treated to a long-overdue modernisation.

World War I

On 18 August 1914, the Australian Naval and Military Expeditionary Force left Sydney for German New Guinea. The troops became the first Australian troops to join the fighting of World War I. The conflict that was to drag on for four years, and some 60,000 of the 330,000 Australian servicemen who fought overseas were killed. As was the case elsewhere in the world, the post-war period was a time of innovation – Sydney's underground railway opened in 1926 and the England-Australia Telephone Service logged its first calls in 1930 – but this was followed by the Great Depression. In Australia, the debate on unemployment developed into a class war. Jack Lang's Labor government confronted the right-wing, paramilitary New Guard. The inauguration of the Sydney Harbour Bridge in March 1932 was supposed to be a proud moment for the entire nation, but the New Guard's Captain de Groot took it upon himself to slash the ribbon with his sword before Premier Lang could cut it with due pomp and ceremony.

In 1921, there were some 30,000 cars registered in New South Wales: this figure had risen to more than 625,000 in 1961. (The Sydney tram was an unfortunate casualty of the car's popularity. Although the expression 'shoot through like a Bondi tram' can still occasionally be heard, the last tram completed its final journey in 1961.)

By 1975 the number of automobiles cruising the streets of New South Wales had increased to 1.4 million. Sydney's population was also growing dramatically. The 500,000 total in 1900 had doubled by 1931, and quadrupled by 1961. Now its residents number aproximately four million, making it by far the largest city in the country.

One of the largest influxes of immigrants arrived after World War II. Europeans, especially Italians and Greeks, and their Australian-born children, accounted for more than 75 percent of Sydney's population growth between 1947 and 1971. This and subsequent migrations, more recently from Asia, quickly turned the insular colonial outpost into a multicultural, cosmopolitan city.

The Tallest Building

The city's tallest pre-World War II building was 11 storeys high. In 1961, the AMP insurance company completed its 26-storey building on Circular Quay. Massive crowds flocked to marvel at the views from the top. By 1968, the 50-floor circular tower of Australia Square had become the most fash-

Left: Pitt Street, viewed from King Street, in 1895
Above: British immigrants embarking on a new life in the 1940s

ionable rooftop eyrie. The Sydney Tower on top of Centrepoint is, at 300 metres (1,000ft), currently the city's highest building.

In the late 1960s and early 1970s, Sydney, like Washington, London and Paris, played reluctant host to Vietnam War protest marches. Although Australia sometimes seems removed from international crises, the relative proximity of Vietnam brought home the horrors of war to a significant number of students, fellow travellers and of course the flower-power hippies of that era. In the following years, the city seemed to slip into social somnolence. The 1980s saw the arrival of yuppie culture and the advent of new lifestyles. On 26 January 1988, the city marked the dawn of the third century of white settlement. The 1990s was a decade of much optimism. In 1992, the new harbour car tunnel became the first new harbour crossing in a number of years. And in 1994 the city's airport gained a much-needed third runway. The following year, a new Labor government was elected.

The New Millennium

Sydney's role as host of the 2000 Olympic Games led to massive investment in sporting and related facilities. The state government has spent billions on building Olympic venues, expanding the transport infrastructure and improving the quality of city streets, parks and other public places. The extension of the city's suburban rail line to the domestic and international terminals at Kingsford Smith Airport, just 7km (4 miles) from the centre of the city, greatly improves access by the increasing numbers of business travellers and tourists. Tollways help alleviate traffic congestion to the airport and through the city. The completion of the 100,000-seat Stadium Australia, the Olympics' main venue, in the centre of greater Sydney gives the city a much needed venue for major sporting and other events. No longer is Sydney overawed by the Melbourne Cricket Ground's capacity to seat vast crowds at major events.

Few of the world's great cities are blessed with such favourable portents for the new millennium. Sydney's economy is successfully gearing towards the brave new world of cyberspace, tourism, professional sport and mass-market entertainment. If only a fraction of the energy, imagination and money that has gone into staging the Olympics could be ploughed into improving the city's infrastructure, then Sydney would reaffirm its reputation as one of the world's most livable great cities.

Above: the spectacular Olympics 2000 site at Homebush Bay

HISTORY HIGHLIGHTS

50,000 BC (approximate) The first Aborigines arrive.

29 April 1770 Captain James Cook sails the *Endeavour* into Botany Bay.

August 1786 British home secretary Lord Sydney orders the establishment of a 'colony of thieves' at Botany Bay.

20 January 1788 The First Fleet arrives in Botany Bay.

26 January 1788 The new colony moves to Sydney Cove.

1794 The first road leading out of Sydney is built to Parramatta.

1804 Irish prisoners rise against the government at Vinegar Hill.

1810–1821 Governor Macquarie takes New South Wales from colony to fledgling community. Sydney's population in 1810 numbers 6,156.

1817 Macquarie first uses the word 'Australia' in official correspondence.

1820 Sydney's landmass extends to 2 sq km (1sq mile).

1832 Free settlers are offered assisted passage to the new colony.

1840 Transportation of convicts to New South Wales ceases after a total of 83,000 prisoners had been sent there.

July 1842 Sydney declared a city.

1851 E.H. Hargraves discovers gold near Bathurst.

1861 Sydney's population doubles in 10 years to reach 96,000.

1890–1891 Labour strikes cripple the colony.

1892 Sydney and the other Australian colonies experience a major depression.

1889 Sydney Town Hall opens.

1900 Bubonic plague kills 112.

1 January 1901 Australian Federation. Australia's first governor-general, Lord Hopeton, is sworn in.

18 August 1914 First Australian troops to join World War I leave Sydney for German New Guinea.

1926 The city's underground railway opens.

1930 England–Australia telephone service gives Sydney direct voice contact with London.

1931 Sydney's population passes the 1 million mark.

March 1932 The Sydney Harbour Bridge opens.

May 1942 Three Japanese midget submarines enter Sydney Harbour and torpedo a ferry.

1960 Eight-year-old Graham Thorne has the dubious distinction of becoming Australia's first kidnap-ransom victim.

1961 The last Sydney tram makes its final journey.

1966 Australia's currency changes from pounds, shillings and pence to decimal dollars and cents.

1973 Sydney Opera House is officially opened by Queen Elizabeth II. Novelist Patrick White receives the Nobel Prize for Literature.

1975 Labor prime minister Gough Whitlam is dismissed amid great controversy. People take to the streets in protest.

1979 The long-awaited Eastern Suburbs railway opens.

24 October 1980 Multicultural television station SBS begins transmission in Sydney and Melbourne.

1981 Pat O'Shane, Australia's first Aboriginal law graduate, becomes the first woman to head a New South Wales government department.

26 January 1988 Celebration of Australia's bicentenary.

August 1992 The Sydney Harbour Tunnel opens.

September 1993 Formal agreement that Sydney will host the 2000 Olympic Games.

November 1994 A third runway opens at the airport, amid great controversy over aircraft noise.

April 1995 A state Labor government is elected.

December 1995 Glebe Island Bridge, Australia's longest, opens.

May 1998 Public protests at apartment development on the harbour foreshore beside the Opera House.

September 2000 Sydney hosts the new millennium's first Olympic Games.

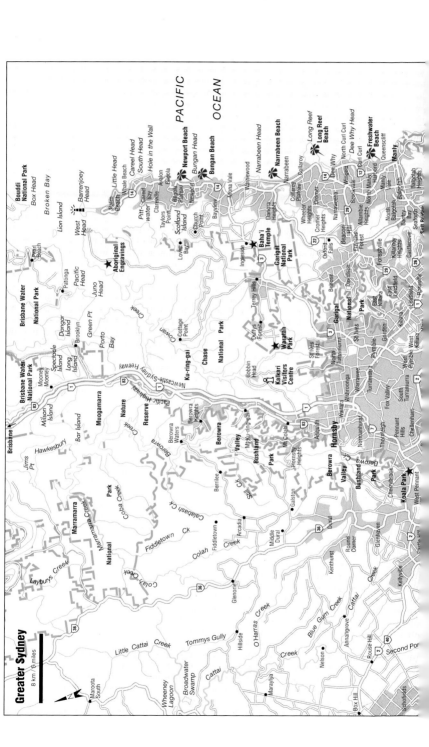

Greater Sydney

8 km / 5 miles

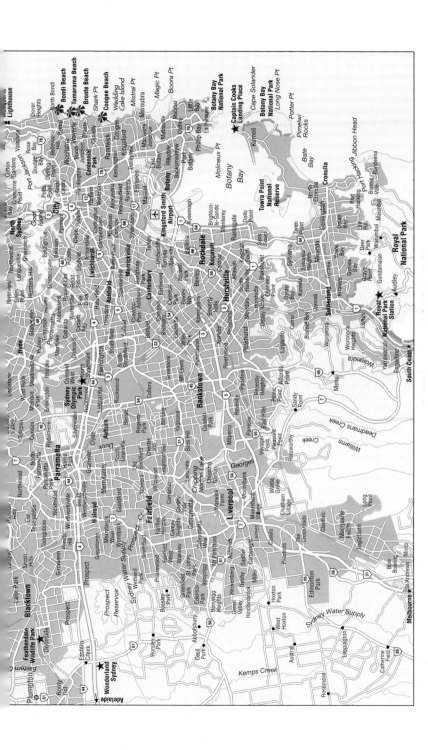

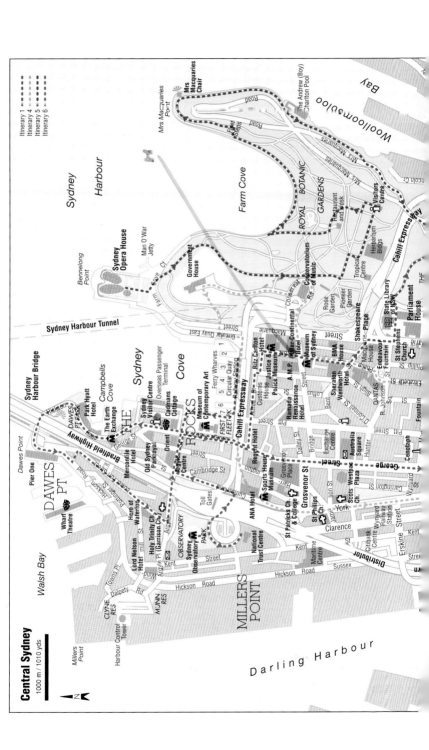

Central Sydney

1000 m / 1010 yds

Itinerary 1
Itinerary 4
Itinerary 5
Itinerary 6

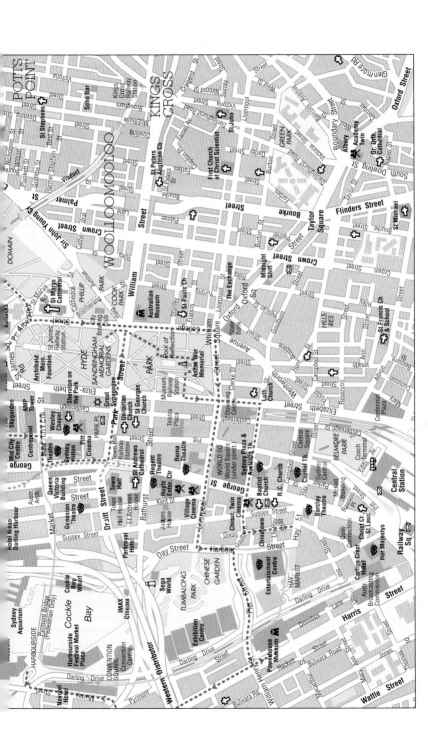

Ci
Itineraries

y itineraries

1. CITY HIGHLIGHTS (see map, p20–21)

The best way to do this walking tour of Sydney's central business district is on foot. Start where the pioneers of the First Fleet did at Circular Quay, turn west along the promenade to the historic Rocks. A walk up George Street will bring you to the shopping arcades, a breath of fresh air at Hyde Park, and then on to Chinatown. Other highlights, including the city's architecture, both historic and modern, the Opera House and museums and art galleries, are covered in Itineraries 4, 5 and 6.

Circular Quay, known originally as Sydney Cove, is where the European settlement of Australia began on 26 January 1788. Today the quay is a terminal for most of Sydney's harbour ferry services, and for buses to the eastern and inner western suburbs, while the railway station on the city circle line serves the western suburbs. The Cahill Expressway and high-rise office developments have obliterated most traces of the quay's colourful history. The 1960s office buildings on the eastern side of the quay have been replaced with colonnaded 'post-modern' apartment blocks and shops. Critics of the 'Toaster', as the block closest to the Opera House has been dubbed, ran a political campaign to have it demolished before it was completed.

Writers Walk

The **Customs House**, the only significant 19th-century building to survive, has been treated to a spectacular revamp and now hosts galleries and exhibitions (daily 10am–5pm; tel: 9247 2285). Crowds of commuters and tourists, entertained by buskers, throng the quay's harbour-side promenade between Bennelong Point and the Rocks. A Writers Walk encircling the quay honours famous Australian authors, with plaques giving details of their careers and works. First Fleet Park on the western side of the quay is a place to rest and watch the crowd's endless bustle, and the ferries coming and going.

The **Rocks** is a short walk west of Circular Quay. Soon after settlement, a collection of wharves, warehouses, hovels, brothels and grog shops sprang up on the sandstone peninsula overlooking Sydney Cove. Grace Karskens' *The Rocks: Life in Early Sydney* (1997) describes everyday life in the Rocks during the convict era. In the mid-19th century, terrace houses for sea captains, merchants and tradesmen were built higher up the cliff on tiers of narrow streets linked by steep sandstone steps.

Left: one of the world's most livable great cities
Right: street entertainer and friend on Circular Quay

By the end of the century, much of the Rocks was a warren of crumbling houses and boarding houses inhabited by the very poor, and seedy pubs frequented by seamen, wharfies, prostitutes, criminals and the notorious 'larrikins of the push'. An outbreak of bubonic plague in the Rocks early in the 20th century led to a government clean up and the demolition of many of the worst hovels. Another 800 houses were demolished in the 1920s to prepare the ground for the approaches to the Harbour Bridge. The Rocks narrowly escaped complete levelling in the 1960s to make way for a high-rise megalopolis when residents enlisted the support of building unions to ban the development. The renovation and preservation of the Rocks began in the 1970s and gathered pace in time for Sydney's bicentennial celebrations in 1988.

The Oldest Residence

Begin your exploration of the Rocks by visiting the Sydney Visitor Centre at 106 George Street (daily 9am–6pm; tel: 9255 1788). The Centre occupies the Sailors Home, built in 1864 to give sailors cheap, clean accommodation away from the vice and crime of the pubs and brothels. Pick up a self-guide historic-walk brochure or join a walking tour. Cadman's Cottage, just south of the Sailors Home, is Australia's oldest residence. Built in 1815 to house the governor's boat crew, captained by the convicted horse thief John Cadman, this small stone building now houses the Sydney Harbour National Park Information Centre (daily 9am–5pm; tel: 9247 5033). Suez Canal, just behind George Street, is typical of the narrow lanes of the Rocks.

Susannah Place in Gloucester Street (Sat–Sun, 10am–5pm, Tues–Wed for bookings; tel: 9241 1893) is a good example of the better, middle-class housing built high on the Rocks. The four Irish-style brick terrace houses, one containing a corner shop, were built in 1844 and now form part of a museum documenting domestic life and architecture in the Rocks. The Merchants House, built in 1842 in the Greek Revival style at 43 George Street for a firm of plumbers and glaziers, is not open to the public.

Campbells Storehouses dominate tiny Campbells Cove. Robert Campbell arrived from India in 1798 to explore the commercial prospect offered by this colony of convicts. He found a strong demand for rum, tobacco, tea and sugar, but trade was hampered by the lack of exports. Campbell prudently bought land at Campbells Cove in 1799. The prosperity of the 1830s, following decades of fluctuating fortunes, allowed Campbell and Company to begin work on the storehouses in 1839. The government bought the two-storey stone building in 1890 and added another floor. The Storehouses

Above: Sydney's world-famous Opera House. **Above right**: marking a Rocks revival **Right**: the historic setting of Sydney Cove restaurants

now contain a restaurant complex and craft shops. Nearby is the five star Park Hyatt Hotel with sweeping views of Sydney Cove and the Opera House. Near the hotel is the Dawes Point Park, named after an artillery engineer with the First Fleet, where you can walk under the Harbour Bridge.

Argyle Cut was begun with convict labour to link the Rocks with Millers Point, but was not finished until explosives for blasting came into use later in the 19th century. The **Argyle Stores** on the eastern side, built as warehouses around a courtyard, contain the Argyle Department Stores (tel: 9251 4800) selling locally designed clothes and assorted home wares. The **Rocks Market** (weekends only; tel: 9255 1717) offers a range of locally made fashion, jewellery and crafts.

From here head south, along George Street into the centre of Sydney, until you get to the **Strand Arcade** (412 George Street, tel: 9232 4199). With its tiered mezzanines and decorative ironwork, this is another venerable, still beautiful, architectural gem. The building connects George and Pitt streets (between King and Market streets). Quality jewellers, watchmakers and fashion designers trade cheek-by-jowl with coffee houses and gift shops, but for many visitors the real attraction is the building itself. A visit to the Strand is a reminder of Australia's early links with London.

Sydney Tower

Walk through the Strand Arcade and emerge in the Pitt Street Mall, where the modern **Skygarden** (tel: 9231 1811) is a money trap disguised as an architectural wonder. Check out the Observation Deck at the **Sydney Tower** (daily 9am–10.30pm except Sat, 9.30am–11.30pm; tel: 9229 7444), taking in a panoramic vista of Sydney from its 300 metres (1,000 ft) vantage point. Entry is from the podium level of the **Centrepoint** shopping centre (corner of Market, Pitt and Castlereagh streets). Take the lift to the top.

Next stop is the **Queen Victoria Building (QVB)**, which occupies a

city itineraries

whole block of George Street to the harbour side of the Town Hall. Its rags-to-riches refurbishment in 1986 transformed its image to the extent that it can be described as the Cinderella of Sydney architecture: an exquisite 19th-century grand design in stone and stained glass. Almost 200 quality shops line the mezzanine galleries. It's a great place to wander, complete with silly clock on the ceiling and a stupendous Chinese jade carriage on the top floor. On the lowest level, 'Eat Street' has limited seating for reasonably priced fast food. Leave the QVB's Victorian grandeur by tunnelling out of its lower depths to the Town Hall railway station or to any other street exit. It is always a surprise to see where you'll pop up.

Hyde Park

After a spot of retail therapy, head for **Hyde Park** on Elizabeth Street. The Scottish troopers who cleared and levelled what had been common grazing land named this inner-city haven after London's famous park. Originally, the park was put to popular use as a racecourse. In 1810 W.C. Wentworth rode Gig in the inaugural Ladies Cup, winning a purse of £50 for his father. A feature of the park today is the canopy of mature trees over the pathways, many of them home to the possums that run around on the lawns.

The Archibald Fountain at the northern end of Hyde Park is named after the co-founder of the *Bulletin*, who left the money for the fountain in his will. Designed by the French sculptor Francois Sicard, the neoclassical bronze and granite fountain commemorates the alliance of Australian and French forces in World War I. The pergola of the sunken Sandringham Garden, a memorial to kings George V and VI near the corner of Park and College streets, is a cascade of flowering wisteria during September. The Art Deco ANZAC Memorial and Pool of Remembrance (daily 9am–4.30pm; tel: 9267 7668) at the southern end of Hyde Park commemorates the Australians

Above: the Queen Victoria Building

city itineraries

killed in war. Downstairs is a photographic and artefacts exhibition. Stroll down Elizabeth Street and turn right into Goulburn Street. This is the least glamorous, and often most interesting part of town. Soon you'll reach **Dixon Street** and you'll know you're in the heart of **Chinatown**. The 200 metres/yards of Dixon Street from Goulburn to Hay streets are the symbolic and tourist centre of this long-established cultural pocket.

Chinatown

The city's first Chinatown was in the Rocks. In the 1850s, thousands of Chinese immigrants arrived en route to the gold fields. Chinese traders rented ramshackle buildings in the Rocks as shops, eating and lodging houses, and opium dens. In the 1870s, Chinese shopkeepers, fruit-and-vegetable merchants and tradesmen plied wares near the Belmore Markets, now the site of the Capitol Theatre at 13 Campbell Street, Haymarket. When the Central Markets were constructed on the swampy upper reaches of Darling Harbour in the 1920s, Chinese greengrocers moved to Dixon Street, one of a maze of narrow, winding streets on the markets' eastern fringe. Chinese shops, restaurants, clubs and gambling dens followed as Dixon Street became the Chinese community's commercial and social hub.

With the end of the 'White Australia' policy in the1960s, Chinese immigrants from Malaysia, Hong Kong and Singapore began settling in Sydney, many with substantial capital to invest. Those accustomed to the excitement and intensity of inner city life in Hong Kong or Singapore moved into new high-rise apartment blocks in or near Chinatown. The transformation of Dixon Street into a tourist attraction began in 1979 when it was closed to traffic, paved, and decorated with ceremonial gateways, planter boxes with Chinese plants, and an octagonal pavilion. The ceremonial gate at the north end of Dixon Street carries the inscription: 'Carry the past into the future'.

There's no better way to end the tour than with a Chinese meal – you probably have no alternative. Restaurants with plate glass and marble facades – the Golden Harbour (tel: 9212 5987), Eastern August Moon (tel: 9212 1899), Nine Dragons (tel: 9211 3661), Noble Dragon (tel: 9211 3682) – occupy Dixon Street at street-level, alongside banks, currency exchanges, jewellers, and souvenir and craft shops. Experience a sense of Dixon Street in the 1960s at the Hingara Restaurant (tel: 9212 2169).

Above: Hyde Park's Archibald Fountain
Left: taming the lion

2. BEACHES, BAYS AND THE INNER EAST *(see map, below)*

Take in the cosmopolitan eastern suburbs of Woolloomooloo, Potts Point, Double Bay and Vaulcuse, Sydney's beaches, from Bondi to Coogee, the new Fox Australia Studios and theme park at Centennial Park, and the inner-city restaurants and dance clubs of Oxford Street.

The best way to see these sights is to catch the Bondi and Bay Explorer at Circular Quay. You can alight at any of the stops listed, stay as long as you wish, and then board the next available bus.

Catch the bus from **Circular Quay**. (For all enquiries about the route ring the Bus, Rail and Ferry Infoline on 131500.) Hop off at **Woolloomooloo**, a rapidly changing bayside enclave tucked between the bustle of the city and the sophistication of Potts Point. Once a neighbourhood of fishermen and wharfies, and still packed with 19th-century terraces, Woolloomooloo has since been renovated with council housing. Higher income folk occupy the district's new town houses and apartment buildings. The massive old timber finger wharf jutting into the bay was built in the early 1900s and served as a passenger terminal and commercial wharf for many years. This once creaking, rat-infested structure has great character and is well on its way to becoming the apartment complex that will redefine the concept of a harbour view.

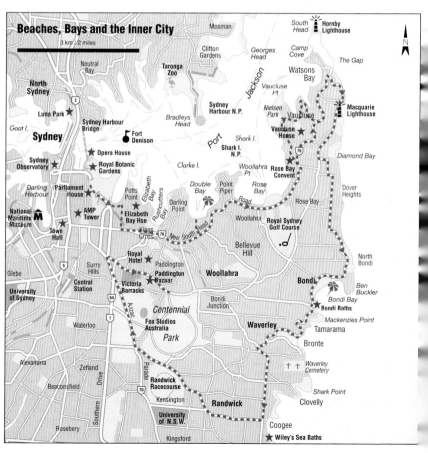

Beaches, Bays and the Inner City

3 km / 2 miles

Harry's Café de Wheels (tel: 9357 3074), a mobile van parked on Cowper Wharf Road, has long been famous for its 'floaters' – meat pies topped with a scoop of blue peas. The **Garden Island naval base** at the end of Cowper Wharf Road is Australia's largest fleet base. It has many historic buildings and a garden that marks the site of the colony's first garden. (Governor Phillip had it planted for the exclusive use of officers of the First Fleet.) This section of the base, the northern tip, was opened to the public in June 2000 (details from the Sydney Visitor Centre, tel: 9255 1788).

Potts Point and Elizabeth Bay

Look out for the **McElhone Stairs** (113 of them), up which you can climb to **Potts Point**. Victoria Street, canopied by plane trees in summer, has views across Wolloomooloo Bay to the city, as well as some of Sydney's most imposing Victorian terraces, and a range of restaurants and cafés. In the 19th century, Potts Point and Elizabeth Bay were home to some of Sydney's wealthiest families, but only a few of their stately mansions, including Tusculum Villa and Rockwall, have survived. **Elizabeth Bay House** at 7 Oslow Avenue (Tues–Sun 10am–4.30pm; tel: 9356 3022) is a Georgian mansion designed by John Verge and built for the colonial secretary in 1839. The internal staircase, sweeping up from an oval saloon beneath a domed ceiling, is one of Australia's most beautiful. The house is fully furnished in the style of the period. Make time for a walk around the streets of Potts Point and Elizabeth Bay to see the magnificent apartment blocks dating from the turn of the century through to the 1930s. Such old-style apartments, particularly of such density, are very rare in Australia – the land of the quarter-acre plot.

The Explorer (pick it up in Bayswater Road) takes you through the fabulously wealthy suburb of Darling Point into **Double Bay**, heartland of eastern suburbs café society. Knox Street, off New South Head Road, has more than a dozen outdoor restaurants, cafés, hotels and boutiques in less than 200 metres/yards). Walk along Bay Street to Double Bay Park on the harbour.

From Double Bay, the Explorer proceeds along New South Head Road, past Redleaf Pool and Point Piper, to the majestic sweep of Rose Bay. Alight at **Rose Bay Convent**, built

Above: Harry's Café de Wheels
Right: topping up a tan on Bondi Beach

in the style of a French château, for sweeping views of the Harbour Bridge. Walk down Bayview Hill Road to pick up the **Hermitage Foreshore Walk**, a track along the harbour's edge, to Nielsen Park. The **Nielsen Park** beach is one of the prettiest in Sydney, and has the added bonus of a shark-proof net for safe swimming in the harbour, and a kiosk for refreshments. A circular walk through the bushland of Vaucluse Point gives views across the harbour to Clifton Gardens and Georges Head.

Vaucluse House

Just a few minutes from Nielsen Park, **Vaucluse House** (Tues–Sun 10am–4.30pm; tel: 9388 7922) is one of Australia's most significant historical estates, set in a superb sweep of landscaped grounds and gardens. The house, a pot-pourri of architectural styles with Gothic Tudor predominating, was once described as 'a cross between an Indian bungalow and a fortified Scottish manorhouse'. W. C. Wentworth, the leading New South Wales politician in the first half of the 19th century, bought the estate in 1827 and continued to refurbish it into the 1860s. The house gives a fascinating insight into the domestic habits of rich colonials.

From Vaucluse House the Explorer proceeds to **Watsons Bay**. The sights of Watsons Bay, featured in the 'Sydney Harbour Cruises' itinerary, might best be explored by ferry. From Dover Heights, the Explorer descends to the sweeping crescent of **Bondi Beach**, the attractions of which are obvious at a glance. After a day of surf, sun and sand, you can wine and dine at any of the dozens of cafés, restaurants, fish-and-chip shops and pubs that line Campbell Parade and adjacent streets.

In the winter months, you might take the three-hour coastal walk to **Coogee** and its sheltered beach. The walk starts at the Bondi Baths (tel: 9310 4804) – home to the Bondi Icebergs – at the southern end of the beach, traversing headlands, beaches, coves and the historic **Waverley Cemetery** on the cliffs above the breakers. If three hours on foot is too daunting, pick up the Explorer at Bronte Beach. The historic Wiley's **Sea Baths** in Neptune Street (tel: 9665 2838), venue for the first Australian Swimming Championships in 1911 and rebuilt in the 1980s, retain much of their original character. The Coogee Bay Hotel (tel: 9665 0000) on the beach is a popular place for a rocking, roisterous night.

Above: Bondi Promenade. **Left**: Bondi Pavilion mural
Right: the view from the Manly ferry

From Coogee the Explorer returns to the city via Randwick Raceco
and Fox Studios Australia in Driver Avenue on the site of the old Ro
Agricultural Society's Showground at Centennial Park. Beyond its sound
stages, **Fox Studios** offers the Backlot movie theme park (10am–6pm
daily; tel: 9383 4000), the Comedy Store, 16 cinemas, boutiques, a book-
shop and offshoots of some of Sydney's best restaurants – including The
Beach Road from Palm Beach and Chinatown's The Golden Century.

Paddington, constructed along the ridge from Taylors Square to Centennial Park, is the final stop before the city. The Victorian terraces sloping
down to Rushcutters Bay were, until the 1960s, regarded as little more than
slums. Today Paddington's rows of renovated and restored terraces remain
largely intact and are rated as architectural gems – a fact reflected in the
price of real estate here. Paddington also has the city's finest concentration
of art galleries, which sell paintings and sculpture from every period and
style of Australian art. The **Paddington Bazaar** (tel: 9331 2646), the city's
most interesting outlet of its type, is open all day on Saturdays in the
grounds of the church on Oxford Street. Finish your day in the Oxford
Street area. Grab a grill at the famous Balkan just near Taylors Square on
Oxford Street (tel: 9360 4970), or stop for a beer at the historic Royal Hotel
on Five Ways (tel: 9331 2604).

3. SOME SYDNEY HARBOUR CRUISES *(see map, p33)*

**Sydney is a city situated on a harbour that happens to be one of the
world's scenic wonders, and Circular Quay is the gateway to that harbour. A fleet of 27 ferries and high-speed JetCats and RiverCats provide an efficient and – after a hard day at the office – relaxing service
for many thousands of commuters every day.**

Any visitor to Sydney should take a trip to the harbour to see the many sights
and delights of Manly, Cremorne and Mosman, Taronga Park Zoo and Watsons Bay. A trip by ferry on a warm summer's night is a magical experience.

city itineraries

For information on all ferry, Jet-Cat and RiverCat routes and timetables, contact the State Transit Authority, tel: 131500, 6am– 10pm daily, or visit the Transport Information Kiosk at Circular Quay. Private companies also provide special excursions around the harbour. If you're interested in taking a harbour cruise on a replica of Captain Bligh's HMS *Bounty*, phone 9247 1789. Other cruises are offered by Captain Cook Cruises (tel: 9206 1122) and Matilda Cruises (tel: 9247 7377).

The Ferry to Manly

Manly – 'seven miles from Sydney and a thousand miles from care' – is in fact 33 minutes from Circular Quay on a traditional ferry, or 15 minutes by JetCat. The ferry may be slower but it is cheaper and gives you a much better view of the passing harbour-side scenery. Look out for the Opera House, Fort Denison, the Garden Island naval base, the Harbour Bridge, the expensive real estate on Darling Point, Point Piper, Sydney Heads and Middle Harbour with their lighthouses, Balmoral Beach, and the expanses of virgin bushland on the foreshores that have now been incorporated into the Sydney Harbour National Park. The many attractions of the resort-style suburb are detailed in the itinerary The Spit to Manly Harbour Walk (*see page 49*).

A good excursion from Manly is to the **Quarantine Station** in the bushland of **North Head** overlooking the harbour. It was here that, until 1984, immigrants suspected of carrying infectious diseases were kept in isolation. Hour-long tours depart at 1.30pm on Monday, Wednesday, Friday, Saturday and Sunday. A bus leaving Manly Wharf at 1.10pm will get you there in time for the tour. For bookings ring the Sydney Harbour National Park (tel: 9977 6522). From the Quarantine Station, a short walk brings you to the precipitous heights of North Head, which has some of the most spectacular views of the ocean, harbour, eastern suburbs and the city.

Above: the historic Bounty
Right: riding a reptile at Taronga Zoo

The inner harbour ferries take you to the lower north shore suburbs of **Cremorne** and **Mosman** for walks around the harbour and among federation villas in parkland settings. Take the ferry to Cremorne Point, follow the footpath along the western side of Mosman Bay for about 30 minutes and catch a ferry at Mosman Wharf back to Circular Quay. A much longer and more strenuous walk begins at the Taronga Park Wharf along the shoreline past Bradleys Head, and through the Sydney Harbour National Park to the charming harbourside reserve of **Clifton Gardens**. On the walk up to Middle Head Road you pass some of Sydney's best federation-style houses.

Taronga Zoo

Taronga Zoo (9am–5pm daily; tel: 9969 2777) is a 15-minute ferry ride from Circular Quay. You can then take a cable-car to the top of the zoo. The setting, on a ridge of natural bushland overlooking the harbour, is virtually unrivalled. Australia's indigenous animals – kangaroos, wallabies, koalas, wombats, platypuses, echidnas – are on display, as well as many species of birds, such as kookaburras, galahs and parrots, and of course the country's dangerous reptiles. You can buy refreshments and enjoy a picnic on a grassy strip looking south over the harbour – *taronga* is an Aboriginal word for 'water view' – and the city. Follow the winding paths between the exhibits down to the ferry wharf at the end of your visit.

Watsons Bay, once a fishing village just inside South Head, is one of Sydney's most picturesque suburbs and a popular harbourside attraction. Walk down Cliff Street to **Camp Cove** where, on summer days, the beautiful people of the eastern suburbs display themselves, then take the track that leads to South Head. Follow the track across the cliffs to the Gap and Dunbar Head, named after a migrant ship driven on to rocks during a gale in 1857 with the loss of 121 lives. On the way back to the wharf, explore the

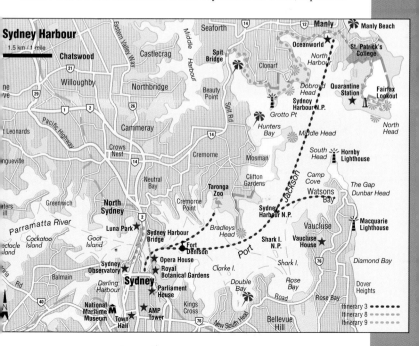

narrow streets with their renovated fishermen's cottages. While waiting for a ferry to take you back to Circular Quay, you can replace those lost fluids and calories with a few refreshing ales in the Watsons Bay (Doyles) Hotel beer garden (1 Military Road; tel: 9337 4299) or fish and chips at Doyles on the Beach (11 Marine Parade; tel: 9337 2007), Sydney's most famous seafood restaurant. Details of ferry and RiverCat services west of the Harbour Bridge are included in the excursion Sydney's West (*see page 69*).

Harbour Islands

Sydney Harbour National Park comprises a collection of scattered reserves, land formerly used by governments for quarantine and defence establishments, and five harbour islands – Fort Denison, Goat, Shark, Clark and Rodd, on the harbour foreshores. The Sydney Harbour National Park Information Centre at Cadmans Cottage (110 George Street; tel: 9247 5033) conducts tours to Goat Island and Fort Denison. Tours depart from Cadmans Cottage on Mondays, Fridays and Saturdays at 1pm; Sundays at 1.30pm. There is also a Sunday picnic tour departing at 11.30am and a 'Gruesome Tales' tour for adults only at 6pm on Saturdays.

In former times, **Goat Island** served as a bubonic plague research station, a port services depot and a shipyard. The land was handed over to the New South Wales National Parks and Wildlife Service in 1994. **Fort Denison** was built in 1857 on an islet to repel potential Russian invaders. The islet, just east of Bennelong Point – now the site of the Opera House – was originally known as Pinchgut because convicts sent there as a punishment subsisted on bread and water. The decaying bodies of executed criminals were displayed on Pinchgut as a warning to passengers on passing ships of the perils of crime. After recent renovations, including a new café, Fort Denison reopened in May 2000 for daily tours. After your day on the water, drop into The Rocks for a meal or a drink, or stroll into the city to catch a film along the movie corridor of George Street.

4. SYDNEY ARCHITECTURE *(see map, p20–21)*

This tour provides an overview of some of Sydney's finest architecture. It would take an entire book to cover every major period and style in a city where rapid growth has resulted in a highly eclectic urban landscape, so the tour is limited to the most interesting highlights.

Travel northwards along Macquarie Street, taking in Circular Quay, the town hall and a few detours. Finish the tour with a meal in one of the inner city's pockets of multiculturalism.

Start off at **St Mary's Catholic Cathedral** (Mon–Fri 6.30am–6.30pm, Sat 8am–7.30pm, Sun 6.30am–7.30pm; tel: 9220 0400), Cathedral Square. Located on the corner of College and Cathedral streets, this magnificent building was designed by the Anglican William Wardell in a 14th-century Gothic style that was popular in the mid- to late 19th century. Wardell, who also designed St Patrick's in Melbourne, was one of the world's greatest proponents of this style. The cathedral, dating from 1885, has always been an important symbol to the Irish community that until the 1960s formed something of an underclass, despite its numbers and influence in fields such as left-wing politics.

Hyde Park Barracks

Next stop is **Hyde Park Barracks** (daily 9.30am–5pm; tel 9223 8922) on Macquarie Street. The building, completed in 1819, is considered one of the architect Francis Greenway's finest works. Greenway was transported for 14 years for forgery in 1814, but his talents were soon recognised by Governor Macquarie – something of a visionary himself when it came to planning and architecture. Greenway's work was admired to the extent that his portrait appeared on Australia's $10 note – probably the only time the image of a convicted forger has appeared on a country's currency. The barracks were built as a prison; there hadn't previously been a jail in the colony as the landscape was deemed deterrent enough. Over its history it has served as a court, a lunatic asylum and a home for single women. It is now a museum, and its exhibits recall the misery of convict life, and the building's history.

The next three buildings, the **Mint**, **Sydney Hospital** and **Parliament House**, occupy the site of Sydney's first hospital – the Rum Hospital. The hospital's origins exemplify the city's creative business practices: three merchants agreed to fund the venture in return for a monopoly on the importation of rum, the most precious currency of the time. The deal went ahead, but the workmanship was so shoddy that the main part of the building (now Sydney Hospital) had to be rebuilt in the 1880s. The hospital's two wings were eventually requisitioned to serve as the Mint and Parliament House. Both wings have undergone considerable renovation, but re-

Left: Doyles seafood restaurant. **Above**: a plaque marking Rum Hospital, the city's first. **Right**: New Parliament House

tain features dating back to 1811. When Parliament is in recess, it's open to the public for tours (9.30am, 11am, 11.45am, 2pm, 2.45pm); when Parliament is sitting, you can watch the proceedings in one of the two chambers (upper and lower, red and green – as at London's Westminster) from the public galleries (tel: 9230 2111).

Chifley Tower

Opposite Sydney Hospital, there are stunning art deco office buildings on **Martin Place**, such as the Commonwealth Savings Bank building between Castlereagh and Elizabeth streets. Finished in 1928, it has been described as 'a sumptuous Beaux-Arts building of immense civic presence'. The interior was lavishly restored during the 1980s. Take a look (weekdays) at the two-storey marble banking chamber. Walk down Elizabeth Street to reach **Chifley Tower** on the corner of Hunter Street. Built at a cost of almost $1 billion, it is, somewhat ironically, named after Ben Chifley, the no-frills Socialist prime minister of the late 1940s. The design, by a Chicago firm, reflects the romantic stylism of early 20th-century American skyscrapers.

The building is colonnaded at street level, opening on to a generous piazza. An up-market shopping arcade and a food court occupy the first three levels. The extensive view east from the top of Chifley Tower can be admired from a table at the expensive restaurant Forty One (tel: 9221 2500).

From Hunter Street, turn into Phillip Street to visit the **Museum of Sydney** complex on the corner of Phillip and Bridge streets. Developed in the mid-1990s, the site incorporates two modern office towers, two rows of historic terrace houses, the Museum of Sydney and the excavated remains of old

Above: Government House
Right: a Botanic Gardens statue

Government House, which dates back to the colony's earliest days. The totem sculptures on the western side of the entrance plaza tell how the Eora people of Sydney suffered at the hands of the Europeans. Be sure to see the fascinating displays within the museum (daily, 9.30am–5pm; tel: 9251 5888) and, if it's a weekday, have a look at the office towers' magnificent foyers.

Loop back to Macquarie Street and stroll among the sheltering palms to the **Conservatorium of Music**, designed by Greenway to serve as Government House stables. This caused an outrage: it was thought an absurdly lavish structure in which to house horses. It has been closed for renovations, but you can get a good look from the outside. Turn left into the driveway through the Royal Botanic Gardens to Government House (grounds open daily 10am–4pm, tours Fri, Sat, Sun 10am–3pm; tel: 9931 5222). Designed by English architect Edward Blore, this Romantic mock castle was built between 1837 and 1845, with the porte-cochère (carriage entrance) added in 1873. The Labor premier decided in 1996 that **Government House** was too grand for a governor – the incumbent was sent packing to his beachside bungalow. The viceregal quarters now form a museum open to the public.

City Exhibition Space

Walk along Circular Quay East to **Customs House** (daily, 10am–5pm; Alfred Street; tel: 9247 2285). Dating from 1885, this building stands on the site where, reputedly, the Union Jack was first flown in Sydney. The building's award-winning interiors have been modernised to create a series of exhibition spaces, including the City Exhibition Space (tel: 9242 8555), charting Sydney's breathtaking rate of growth, and the Djamu Gallery (tel: 9320 6429), part of the Australian Museum collection, which showcases the region's indigenous culture.

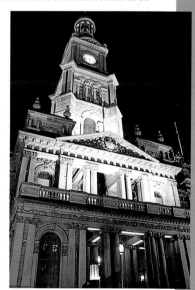

Take a train from Circular Quay to Town Hall to finish the tour. The **Town Hall** (ground floor open 8am–6pm Mon–Fri; tel: 9265 9333, or for tours: 8223 3815) on the corner of Park and George streets, was built on the site of a cemetery. Opened in 1889, its startling mixture of styles reflects the attempts of its six architects to outdo each other in terms of ornate detailing – such was the Victorian era. Next door is **St Andrew's Anglican Cathedral** (daily; tel: 9265 1661), built more on the scale of a large English parish church than a cathedral. Consecrated in 1868, it commemorates early Protestant settlers. From here walk to Liverpool Street and snack on *tapas* at one of the many Spanish restaurants of the Latin Quarter, or venture a little further into Chinatown and treat yourself to an inexpensive meal of noodles in one of Dixon Street's food halls.

This tour is a comfortable half day on foot. From Circular Quay, the Opera House is a five-minute stroll north along the promenade. Take a tour of the Opera House and then visit the Botanic Gardens, where the environments range from tropical rainforest to a desert cactus garden, all set against the incomparable backdrop of Sydney Harbour.

The passing of Sydney's tram age facilitated the building of one of the 20th century's great architectural masterpieces, the **Sydney Opera House**. In 1947 Sydney Symphony Orchestra conductor Eugene Goossens suggested that the

city should have an opera house. The tram depot at Fort Macquarie on Bennelong Point closed in 1956, leaving an ideal site vacant. An international contest to design the building was won by Danish architect Joern Utzon. Rumour has it that his radical design was thrown out, but an American judge, arriving late, plucked Utzon's plan from the reject pile and said, 'Gentlemen, here is your opera house.'

Timeless Synergy

Utzon's concept of two sail-like structures covered with white ceramic tiles, suggestive of yachts on the harbour, generated an international controversy. Traditional architectural forms seemed to have no bearing on the design. The roof, covered with a million anti-fungal tiles, and weighing 158,000 tons, dominates the walls, and there is none of the traditional visual emphasis on windows, columns and pediments. Utzon achieved a timeless synergy between the organic shape of the Opera House and its harbour setting, almost as if, as one commentator has suggested, 'the scheme actually involved flooding the harbour valley to set the building off to its best advantage.' Construction encountered a number of engineering and budget problems that forced the government to scale the project down. Utzon resigned in protest and a Sydney firm was commissioned to redesign his exotic interior. The original estimate of $7 million had become $102 million by the time the building was completed; government lotteries paid for most of the bills.

The Queen opened the Opera House in 1973. The first production in the Opera Theatre was Prokofiev's *War and Peace* and in the concert hall Beethoven's *Ninth Symphony*. Today, more than 3,000 performances and events are held annually. The Opera Theatre seats only 1,547. It does not have a big stage or orchestra pit, but does offer an intimate atmosphere. The concert hall seats 2,690 under a vaulted roof for classical, jazz, folk and pop concerts. The 10,500-pipe organ, designed and built by Ronald Sharp, is the world's largest mechanical-action organ. The sumptuous Australian-

Above: the Opera House's magnificent harbour setting
Right: Fig tree in the Botanic Gardens

wood panelling and 18 acoustic rings above the stage reflect the sound. The Drama Theatre seats 550, the Playhouse 398. There is a Green Room, complete with bar, restaurant and lounge, five rehearsal studios, and 60 dressing rooms and suites (guided tours and general enquiries, tel: 9250 7111). The booking office is open Mon–Sat, 9am–8.30pm (tel: 9250 7777).

Opera House Restaurants

The Opera House has several restaurants. The three-level **Bennelong** (tel: 9250 7548), located in the smallest shell in front of the Concert Hall, serves modish local food and wine on the lowest level. The **Crustacea** and **Cocktail** bars on the upper levels serve more casual fare. The **Mozart Café** at the entrance to the Bennelong is for light meals and snacks. **The Concourse** (tel: 9250 7300) under the western forecourt, and **Harbour Restaurant** (tel: 9250 7191), at the tip of Bennelong Point, have indoor and outdoor tables and mezzanine views of the harbour; both offer straightforward menus at moderate prices. The foyer shop and stores along the lower concourse sell CDs, posters, opals, children's clothes and gifts.

The **Monumental Steps** down to the forecourt are a popular venue for meetings, rallies and outdoor performances, especially on sunny winter afternoons and balmy summer nights. At the foot of the Steps, turn left and walk 100 metres/yards to the **Royal Botanic Gardens** through Queen Elizabeth II Gate. The gardens' 30 hectares (74 acres) loop around Farm Cove, or Woccanmagully as the Aborigines called it. The colony's first farm and the governor's kitchen garden became the Botanical Gardens in 1816. Macquarie appointed Charles Fraser, a soldier, as the first colonial botanist.

Stroll up to the **Herb Garden**, just behind the Conservatorium of Music, where you'll find displays charting the history of herbs. Stonework has been used as the framework for plantings. Look for the spherical sundial and sensory fountain that gushes water when approached. The nearby **Rose Garden**, incorporating a pergola and pavilion, is a haven of peace and harmony. The plantings follow the history and diversity of the rose, with the modern

varieties arranged in colour sequences. The magnificent **Tropical Centre's** collection of strange species is spread across two modern glasshouses with climate-control systems that keep the humidity above 75 percent. The **Pyramid** contains native Australian tropical species, while the **Arc** displays exotic tropical species.

Palm Grove

Nearby lies the **Palm Grove**, one of the oldest and most established features of the garden – palms were highly valued for their ornamental and exotic properties in the 19th century. There are nearly 150 species and thousands of plants thriving in a setting that suggests a Victorian painter's version of the Garden of Eden. Near the Palm Grove, the re-creation of the colony's first farm is worth seeing. Opposite the shop and visitors' centre, take another geographical leap in the **Succulent Garden** – this time to the deserts of South Africa and the Americas – for the collection of cactuses and other adapted species.

Drop into the visitor centre and garden shop (daily 9. 30am–4pm; tel: 9231 8125) in the old Herbarium building, just east of the First Farm. The garden shop stocks books on horticulture and gardens, travel guides, prints, souvenirs and gifts. A trackless train tours the gardens with commentary at regular intervals. The **National Herbarium**, the principal centre for botanical research in New South Wales, holds about a million dried-plant specimens, including some collected by Sir Joseph Banks in 1770.

The **Lower Gardens** occupy five hectares (12 acres) reclaimed from Farm Cove. Here you will find the very best of 19th-century landscaping, complete with formal plantings, framed vistas, ornate statues and a series of picturesque little ponds created by the damming of a small creek. Take a stroll along the sea wall – which keeps the reclaimed land of the area from being swamped by the tides – into the **Domain**, the 30-hectare (72-acre) spread of open parkland abutting the Botanic Garden to the south and east. Along the foreshore you will find the **Fleet Steps**, which were built for the benefit of sailors disembarking from ships at Farm Cove, and, more quixotically, **Mrs Macquarie's Chair**, a ledge that was carved from sandstone to enable Governor Macquarie's wife to sit comfortably while admiring one of the most magnificent harbour views in the world.

Finish your tour at the Botanic Gardens restaurant (daily 12–4pm; tel: 9241 2419) northwest of the First Farm, where you can enjoy lunch on a wisteria-covered veranda overlooking the lakes of the Lower Gardens or, alternatively, grab a quick coffee at the kiosk below.

Above: the Botanic Gardens evolved from the colony's first farm

6. MUSEUMS AND ART GALLERIES *(see map, p20–21)*

Place Sydney's museums and art galleries end to end and they would stretch further than a visitor's attention span. The following are just a few of the most interesting and most conveniently located from which to choose for a morning of cultural saturation.

Observatory Hill, in The Rocks area, is a good starting point for a culture cruise. The city's highest natural point, with a spectacular view of Port Jackson, it was the original site of a windmill (1796), then a half-built fort (1803) and finally, in 1848, a shipping signal station. The signal station survives as the **Sydney Observatory** but the era for studying the little-known southern sky has passed; the city's air pollution now makes serious astronomy virtually impossible. Today it is the **Museum of Astronomy** (daily 10am–5pm; Watsons Road, Observatory Hill; tel: 9217 0485). Most evenings the museum conducts night-sky observation sessions for amateur skywatchers.

On the same hill above The Rocks, Governor Macquarie built a military hospital in 1815. It is now the **National Trust Centre**, and incorporates the **S.H. Ervin Gallery** (Tues–Fri 11am–5pm; Sat and Sun noon–5pm; tel: 9258 0150), one of the city's largest non-commercial galleries, which specialises in the best of Australian figurative art.

Contemporary Art

For contemporary art that is thought-provoking and always fresh, visit the **Museum of Contemporary Art** at 140 George Street (daily except Tues 10am–4pm or 5pm; tel: 9252 4033) in the Circular Quay area. The museum, which features exhibitions of Australian and international contemporary art, is housed in a 1950s mock art deco building on Sydney Harbour. The permanent collection, which includes works by the likes of

Above: Observatory Hill
Right: Sydney Observatory

Warhol and Hockney, began as the private collection of a Dr John Power, who bequeathed it to the state in the hope that Australia would at last have a significant modern art institution, and so it does. Apart from the sensational art, the tone of the place is crisp, intelligent and challenging.

Bush Ranger Memorabilia

Just up the hill from Circular Quay, at the corner of Albert and Phillip streets, is the stately sandstone **Justice and Police Museum** (Sat and Sun 10am–5pm; tel: 9252 1144). Comprising the former Water Police Court (1856), Water Police Station (1858) and Police Court (1886), this little-known museum is the place to see bush-ranger memorabilia, such as Captain Moonlite's death mask and Ben Hall's pistol, and to hear the tale of Constable Alexander Walker's duel to the death with the legendary Thunderbolt. Forensic evidence from notorious crimes, early criminal mug-shots and an assortment of spine-chilling murder weapons are also on display in this chamber of horrors. Visitors can step back in time by participating in a mock trial in a 19th-century police court.

Wander up the hill a further 100 metres/yards and cross over to the corner of Bridge and Phillip streets to discover the terrific **Museum of Sydney** (daily 9.30am–5pm; tel: 9251 5988), recognisable by the Edge of Trees sculpture in its forecourt. Constructed on the site of the first Government House, and incorporating that building's excavated remains, the museum showcases the city's history through fascinating displays of trade, art and architecture. Long-lost characters spring to life through holograms, and a 33-screen video panel highlights the contemporary environment.

A short walk across the Domain parkland from Macquarie Street brings you to the **Art Gallery of New South Wales** (daily 10am–5pm; tel: 9225 1700) in Art Gallery Road. Fronted by an imposing 1909 neoclassical façade with a massive neoclassical portico, this is one of the country's best galleries, with a collection that defies categorisation. Highlights include the Australian Collection, which documents all the major periods in the country's brief but rich art history and includes names such as Boyd, Nolan and Cossington Smith. The Western Art Collection features the likes of Turner,

Caravaggio and Picasso. But the most dynamic collection is Yirbana, which features Aboriginal and Torres Strait Islander work. This is one of the largest collections of indigenous art in the world. The works are fascinating in themselves, and also in the context of the impact colonisation had on Aboriginal culture. They also reveal much about the incorporation of traditional techniques into contemporary work.

If you haven't had a surfeit of museums, continue to **The Australian Museum** (daily 9.30am–5pm; tel: 9320 6000) at the corner of William and College streets. This museum holds the country's largest collection of natural history exhibits, with well-displayed marine life, bird and mammal sections, and an excellent Aboriginal Australia display.

Hands-On Displays

Back across town, just west of Darling Harbour at 500 Harris Street, is the superstar of Sydney museums and the state's prime tourist attraction: the hugely popular **Powerhouse Museum** (daily 10am–5pm; tel: 9217 0111). This 1899 power station and former tram depot has been renovated to house the huge collection of material that the Museum of Applied Arts and Sciences has been accumulating since the 1880s. Visitor participation is encouraged in the many 'hands-on' displays. Exhibits include the state's first train engine, bush kitchens, craft and fashion items, planes and even a space shuttle. The emphasis is on things Australian, although the international context is not lost. Allow plenty of time for the Powerhouse, especially if you have children – kids love it and it loves them.

Darling Harbour is home to two nautical museums, both on the western shore. Beneath the sail-like roofs of the **Australian National Maritime Museum** (daily 9.30am–5pm) is an exciting presentation of the country's long maritime history. There are also numerous commercial art galleries catering to different tastes, from outback kitsch to postmodern obsessive. For $2 you can buy a copy of *Art Almanac*, which provides up-to-date information on what's on where, from most galleries and bookshops.

There are a lot of private galleries in the Paddington-Woollahra area and, increasingly, in the working-class suburbs of the inner-west. The **Brett Whiteley Studio** (Sat and Sun 10am–4pm; 2 Raper Street, Surry Hills; tel: 9225 1881) displays the works of the late, mercurial Australian painter. Whiteley was very much a Sydney artist and his large canvases depict the city in the most sensuous and celebratory of guises.

Left: Jeff Koons's Flower Dog outside the Museum of Contemporary Art
Top: in the Justice and Police Museum. **Above**: sculpture by David Moore

7. DARLING HARBOUR *(see map, p45)*

The most visited of Sydney's harbourside public areas, the Darling Harbour complex can keep you busy for as much time as you have. It is easily reached from the city via the convenient and fast monorail. Once there, you can just wander around and browse, or fill many hours at the Powerhouse Museum… or at the bars.

Darling Harbour has so many facets that each visitor sees it in a different light. To describe it as a collection of shops, restaurants, bars, museums, funfair and marina, plus a convention centre, a huge exhibition hall, a Chinese garden and an entertainment centre on the fringe of the city does not do justice to the sense of identity that it's developing. On Sunday, when the rest of Sydney has largely shut down, Darling Harbour exudes fun and is crowded with locals and visitors alike. *The* success story of Australian urban renewal, it should be seen in its context.

A Promise Kept

For years prior to its redevelopment, Darling Harbour was the city's unwashed sink, an industrial eyesore comprising 50 hectares (123 acres) of railyards, wharves and factories. By the 1970s, these expansive metallic slums were just a hole in the landscape to be ignored while crossing Pyrmont Bridge. In 1984, the state premier promised that the area would be 'reborn' as a bicentennial gift to the people of Sydney in 1988. So a consortium of government and private enterprise tore everything down and built a place for the people, which uses the waterway as a central theme.

One of the most controversial facets of the development is the monorail between the city and Darling Harbour. Detractors claim that it has destroyed Sydney's appearance. Still hoping that it will be torn down, they must enjoy the media's eager coverage of its every breakdown and financial loss. But

Above: Darling Harbour

others find it a most convenient mode of transport. The best place to get information about the complex is the **Sydney Visitor Centre** (daily 10am–6pm; tel: 9286 0111) on the eastern side, not far from Sega World.

Aesthetics aside, in terms of getting to Darling Harbour, and getting around once there, the monorail isn't such a bad choice. Just remember it only travels in one direction – anti-clockwise – so you must plan the order in which you want to visit the attractions, or risk having to go all the way through the loop to get someplace that's only one stop behind you. Then again, you could always walk. A light rail (tram) service runs from Central Railway along the western edge of Darling Harbour and is useful for getting to places such as the Powerhouse, Star City and Sydney Fish Market. The number for both the monorail and the light rail is: 8584 5288.

Crocodiles and Sharks

Alternatively, hop aboard one of the fleet of small vehicles known as 'people movers', which will shuttle you from one spot to the next. This tour starts in the northeast, at the spot nearest the city, and swings around the curve of Cockle Bay to finish in Pyrmont. Start at the **Sydney Aquarium** (daily 9.30am–10pm; tel: 9262 2300) on the city side of the cove. Shaped like a breaking wave, the aquarium contains a good cross-section of the in-

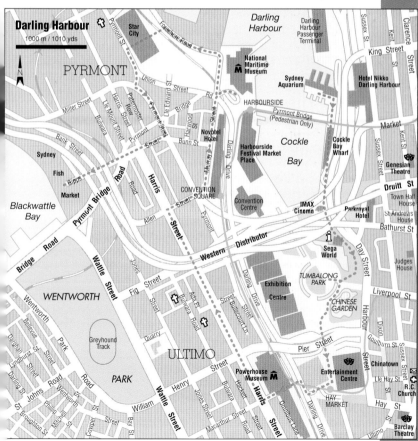

credible range of fish that inhabits Australian waters. There are no crocodiles native to New South Wales waters, but they can be seen here. Sydney certainly does have sharks, however, and you can confront these and other harbour inhabitants nose-to-nose in the aquarium's reassuringly safe transparent tunnel. Visitors to the Australian fur seal enclosure can see these endearing creatures play through underwater viewing windows.

A Public Outcry

Pyrmont Bridge, right beside the aquarium, provides the fastest pedestrian access to Darling Harbour from the city. First built in 1858, the private toll bridge charged pedestrians 'tuppence' each way; sheep and pigs were charged a farthing a head. By the 1880s, the old wooden bridge had outlived its usefulness and the government suggested demolishing it to open up Darling Harbour. (The resulting public outcry was echoed a century later when the government considered tearing down its successor. In neither case did the government go ahead.) Instead, the colonial government bought the bridge and abolished the toll, later replacing the whole structure. When the Pyrmont Bridge that stands today was opened in 1902, the year after the Commonwealth of Australia became a nation, it was a hailed as a wonder that pushed the limits of contemporary engineering. The bridge, with its quaint control box in the middle, is worth seeing, especially when its electronic, 800-tonne, 70-metre (230-ft) 'swing span' pivots horizontally to let large vessels enter the inner harbour.

Just beyond Pyrmont Bridge, you'll find the Cockle Bay Wharf, the newest development on the block. Here the focus is almost exclusively on food. The range of eateries includes one of Sydney's most expensively outfitted restaurants, **Amersand** (tel: 9264 6666), whose menu is best described as a sophisticated blend of French and Japanese – this would make a good choice for a big night out.

Eight-Storey Movie Screen

Next up is **Panasonic Imax** (daily; tel: 9281 3300), one in an international chain of cinemas that provides huge screens – this one is eight storeys high. The films screened are made on a special format to meet the screening conditions, and the quality of the image is really quite extraordinary. Children's movies and adventure documentaries are the standard fare. Try to get a seat in the centre of the cinema; strange things happen to the image the further to the side you go. The cinema is right in front of Cockle Bay, an open-air waterside area where there's always something going on in the way of free entertainment. Aqua-Magic (tel: 1900 957255), a film-and-laser show, is

Above: a resident of Taronga Zoo's koala house. **Above right**: children love Sega World
Right: tranquillity in the Chinese Garden

screened across the water at night. Also close is **The Wockpool** (tel: 9211 9888), a large modern Asian noodle bar. It can be expensive but there are usually some excellent lunch specials.

Further along is **Sega World** (tel: 9273 9273). Opening times depend on school holidays and the like, but usually the complex opens mid-morning and closes between 8pm and 10pm. Ring first to check. This attraction is best described as a giant, indoor, high-tech theme park with virtual rides and futuristic exhibits. Children love it.

Facing Sega World is **Tumbalong Park**, a grassy circle fringed by eucalyptus and tree-lined walks veering into the middle distance. Most of the landscaped vegetation is is indigenous. The park caters for kids of all ages; there is an excellent children's playground and amphitheatre for open-air performances. Buskers and bands perform here, too, particularly on sunny weekends, when it makes a relaxing spot to break your itinerary.

A Gift from China

Next to Tumbalong Park is the **Chinese Garden** (daily 9.30am–5pm; tel: 9281 6863), built as a bicentennial gift by the government of China's Guangdong province. It is found behind high walls, which protect it from the noise pollution of the traffic. Inside, you'll find a peaceful garden refuge of lakes, waterfalls and perfectly executed landscaping. Sydney's climate is similar to that of Guangdong's capital Guangzhou, so many Chinese species were suitable for planting, including four types of bamboo, evergreen pines and willows, the flowering apricot (the national flower of

China) and red silk cotton trees, the floral emblem of Guangdong. In particular, note the floral emblem of New South Wales, the waratah, growing around the Twin Pavilion and carved into its woodwork. Lots of ducks have

taken up residence in the garden's large lakes, and you might also see koi carp swimming among the lotuses and water lilies.

The **Australian National Maritime Museum** (tel: 9552 7777) to the right of Pyrmont Bridge houses all manner of vessels, both as permanent outdoor displays and inside exhibits, that deal with all facets of the Australians' relationship with the sea. There are six different exhibitions within the billowing sail-like structure of local architect Phillip Cox's building. Each focuses on the nation's historical landmarks, in categories such as discovery, commerce, defence and leisure. The most moving exhibition, about human migration, traces the voyages of convicts, free settlers, post-World War II European immigrants and refugees from the Vietnam War. This is one of the largest museums of its kind; don't miss it.

The Desert in the Casino

Just across the way – and you really can't miss it – is **Star City** (daily, 24 hours; tel: 9777 9000), the legal casino that has knocked the life out of what was once Sydney's thriving illegal gambling network. Like so much of Darling Harbour's redevelopment, the battle for the casino was fought in print and across the state's television screens. Sydneysiders relate with self-deprecating glee that the proposed casino was in limbo then canned altogether because the government was simply unable to find anyone honest enough to run it; then the proposal was revived by the following government only to be killed off by crusaders for public morals.

Eventually Star City saw the light of day. Its features include bars, cafés, restaurants, shops, acres of gaming tables and slot machines and the 2,000-seat Lyric Theatre. The complex's interior design draws inspiration from the Australian landscape, so one moment you're in the middle of the desert, the next, the mysterious green depths of the wet tropics. Rumour has it that, after seeing these ersatz environments, impressed tourists have cancelled trips to the real thing on the grounds that they've already experienced it.

Finish your trip at the **Sydney Fish Market** (daily 7am–4pm; corner of Pyrmont Bridge Road and Bank Street, Blackwattle Bay; tel: 9660 1611). This magnificent open-air market sells both fresh and cooked fish. You can cruise the stalls, pick out your choice of oyster or species of fish, and sit down to observe the splendid chaos of Sydney Harbour's industrial precinct.

Above: the National Maritime Museum re-creates the country's discovery

8. THE SPIT TO MANLY HARBOUR WALK *(see map, p33)*

An easy 8-km (5-mile) trail leads around the northern foreshores of Sydney Harbour from Spit Bridge to Manly Wharf. In places, this unparalleled eyeful of Australian bush and bay is much as Captain Arthur Phillip would have seen it back in 1787.

If it's a beautiful, sunny day, put on a pair of light walking shoes and a sunhat, arm yourself with a bottle of water and head out for three hours of coastal walking. **The Spit** – short for 'sandspit' – is located about 30 minutes north of the city, via north Sydney, Neutral Bay, Mosman and Spit Junction. Government buses (tel: 131500) from York Street in the city will get you there, but it will be far quicker to catch a taxi.

After arriving at the northern end of the **Spit Bridge**, cross the road to the eastern side, descend to a grassy clearing, then follow the path east around the foreshore. Generally well marked, the trail becomes temporarily obscure in only one or two places – if so, just retrace your footsteps and look again.

Leaf-framed views of sandstone headlands, views of ultramarine (verging on violet) harbour expanse, sails and ferry wakes, bomboras (reef waves), buoys and picnic coves – all these will delight the hiker. Bring your swimming gear and take a dip from time to time, although in summer you should be mindful of sharks. It has been a quarter of a century since the last fatal attack inside the harbour, but why risk becoming a footnote in history?

As you amble along – and there is no hurry – you will pass the front lawns of a number of sumptuous houses. Odd though it may seem, you will see virtually no birds or fauna, and certainly no kangaroos or koalas. But don't be deterred by this dearth of natural wonders; much of the trail runs through sections of

Above: Manly Cove
Right: bushwalking on the harbour shore

Sydney Harbour National Park. Contact the park's information centre (Cadmans Cottage, 106 George Street, the Rocks; tel: 9247 5033) for an informative guide to the natural and historical aspects of the walk. You can also check out the illustrated plaques along the way. In parts, there is evidence of bushfires: these happen infrequently, and only in high summer – although in 1990 a group of Japanese tourists had the thrill of being rescued from a fire in this area by way of a helicopter evacuation.

Shark-Free Swimming

The first section of the 40-minute walk, a 1.5-km (1-mile) hike to **Clontarf Beach**, skirts a shady bay before arriving at Clontarf, which has shark-proof swimming, picnic facilities and road access. It is possible to cover only portions of this walk, exiting where the trail meets a local road, such as Beatty Street, Balgowlah – although here you'll be a long way from public transportation. Continue on to **Castle Rock** and **Grotto Point**, site of a pretty lighthouse that from afar looks like a tiny Greek-island chapel. Close up, the lighthouse is far less interesting, but its location gives a great view of what Captain Phillip called 'the finest harbour in the world.'

You soon approach the halfway point on the trek, about 3km (2 miles) and 85 minutes later. Nearby are Aboriginal carvings made by a tribe that was wiped out by smallpox in the early days of the colony. These are not signposted for fear of attracting graffiti writers. Easier to spot is **Washaway Beach** below Grotto Point, a nudist beach and a good place for a swim. Next come **Crater Cove**, **Dobroyd Head** (spot the tiny rock huts in the cove – fishermen and drop-outs lived in them for years) and the nudist **Reef Beach**. If you arrive at Reef Beach by boat, watch out for the dangerous swell: regulars keep score of the boats that come ashore capsized.

Above: surveying the Harbour scene
Left: a Sunday juggler at Manly Corso

When you hit **Forty Baskets Beach**, the modest attire of the swimmers signals the end of the 'wild' part of the walk. From here on it's mainly a suburban stroll for the next 30 minutes around the foreshores of **Fairlight Beach**. This potted view of the Australian bush gives way to the leisure possibilities of Manly – so named because Captain Phillip thought the local Aborigines – who eventually speared him – were 'manly'. The highlight of the **Manly Oceanworld** (daily 10am–5.30pm; tel: 9949 2644) on West Esplanade is a moving footway which takes you through a transparent acrylic tunnel above which fish, including sharks, swim. Other attractions in Manly include the **Art Gallery** (Tues–Sun 10am–5pm; West Esplanade; tel: 9949 2435), which features some wonderful work, dating from 1900, dealing with seaside themes. At the end, at Manly Wharf, fairground rides (daily) include a ferris wheel that hangs out over the harbour edge.

Australian Seaside Culture

After a drink at **Manly Wharf**, head east to **The Corso**. This street was named after Corso in Rome, but that is where all similarity ends. Culturally, it is about as far away from the Italian capital as you can get. This is Australian seaside culture: Norfolk pines, fast food, beer drinkers on the pavement, shoeless kids, shirtless men, scantily clad women and so on. The street ends at the Pacific Ocean and the expanse of surf and sand that is **Manly Beach**. Buy seafood from the nearby fish and chippie, and unwrap it beneath the stately Norfolk pines as you watch the surfers and promenaders.

Facing the sea, to your left, at the far end of the beach, is **Queenscliff**, and to your right **Shelly Beach** cove, the point and surf of **Fairy Bower**, and the **North Head** of Sydney Harbour. The Gothic-looking stone building on the hill is **St Patrick's College**. For information about this lovely suburb, go to the **Manly Visitors' Information Bureau** (tel: 9977 1088) at the ocean end of The Corso. If you haven't eaten and you're in the mood for a fresh, unpretentious meal, go south towards the Steyne Surf Club, then around the oceanside path. After five minutes you'll reach **The Bower Restaurant** (7 Marine Parade; tel: 9977 5451). A few minutes later, at Shelly Beach, you will find an expensive beachside restaurant, **Le Kiosk** (Marine Parade; tel: 9977 4122), which is good for seafood, but usually requires advance booking.

Return to Manly by the same route or, if you have time, by taxi, for a quick look at **North Head**, the gem of the Sydney Harbour National Park. **Fairfax Lookout** at the point provides a great view. Back towards Manly, on the harbour side, is the defunct 1833 **Quarantine Station**, which is now administered as a tourist attraction by the NSW National Parks and Wildlife Service. These attractions are described more fully in the chapter 'Sydney Harbour Cruises' (*see page 31*). After this hectic morning, you can return to Circular Quay from Manly Wharf, either quickly by JetCat, or by the more leisurely ferry.

Right: fine views by ferry

9. SYDNEY HARBOUR BRIDGE
TO NORTH SYDNEY *(see map, p33)*

The pedestrian walkway on the eastern side of the Sydney Harbour Bridge is perhaps the city's most under-utilised free tourist attraction: the walk to the north shore is highly memorable, and it puts the enormous scale of the bridge into its true proportion.

If you catch a train or ferry back from Milsons Point/Kirribilli, the return trip can take as little as two hours, but it's better to allocate more time. The best time to take this walk is at dawn, when the rising sun turns the water in the harbour into a creamy liquid gold. The place to start this tour is **Dawes Point Park**, directly under the bridge in The Rocks. From here, you get a daunting worm's-eye view of the monumental structure overhead. Spare a thought for the architects and engineers who stood here in the 1920s and envisaged a span reaching across the deep harbour.

One of the largest arch bridges in the world, **Sydney Harbour Bridge** was built from both ends, starting in 1923 and joining in 1930 at a cost of just under £10 million – the loan which financed it was finally paid off in 1988. The stone pylons are largely decorative and the arch is supported by four huge pins, each 35cm (14in) in diameter and 4 metres (13ft) long. The total weight of steel in the bridge is 53,000 tons. It takes 10 years to repaint – a task that consumes over 30,000 litres (6,600 gallons) of paint (ask Paul Hogan, who used to be a rigger on the bridge).

An Embarrassing Incident

Just as the structure has become an enduring part of the city landscape, the opening ceremony, which took place during the Great Depression in March 1932, has become an embarrassing detail of Australian history. Before State premier Jack Lang could ceremonially cut the ribbon to open the bridge, Captain de Groot of the paramilitary New Guard rode up and slashed it with his sword, declaring the bridge open on behalf of 'the decent

and loyal citizens of New South Wales'. The ribbon was eventually re-tied and the official ceremony continued. The political frame could not be so easily fixed; within months, Lang had been dismissed from office by the governor and the far right of New South Wales politics had prevailed.

To reach the bridge's eastern walkway, walk to Cumberland Street at the top of the Argyle steps off Argyle Street. The **Harbour Bridge Pylon Lookout and Museum** (daily 10am–5pm; tel: 9247 3408) is located in the southeastern pylon of the bridge. Inside, check out the display documenting the building of the bridge and, at the top of a 200-step climb (not for the faint-hearted), a lookout with a wonderful panorama of Sydney. And, for the brave, the fit, the foolhardy and those who don't suffer from vertigo, there is now the chance to scale the arch of the bridge, just as painters, engineers and drunks have done for the past 70 years or so. (Contact Bridge Climb, tel: 9252 0077 for details.) There are day and night climbing tours, lasting for about three hours.

Australian Cuisine

North Sydney is the ever-growing centre for much of the city's media and advertising industries. These high-profile businesses are supported by several up-market shopping centres and stylish restaurants. **Armstrongs Brasserie** (1-7 Napier Street, North Sydney; tel: 9955 2066) serves an array of international dishes often described as modern Australian cuisine.

It's a good brasserie, combining lively decor with imaginative cooking. Or try the **Malaya**, in the old fire station at 86 Walker Street (tel: 9955 4306), which is culturally purer, right down to the rather off-hand service.

After a brisk stroll across the bridge, the best way to end the day is to walk down to **North Sydney Olympic Swimming Pool** (Mon–Fri 5.30am–9pm, Sat and Sun 7am–7pm; Alfred Street, Milsons Point; tel. 9955 2309) almost under the northern end of the bridge. In summer, this is an excellent place to swim and sightsee simultaneously – especially if you swim backstroke. Watch the peak-hour crowds stuck in heavy bridge traffic while you wallow languidly below.

After an invigorating swim, sample one of the harbourfront walks stretching west or east of the pool. Heading east under the Sydney Harbour Bridge, follow the foreshore along little more than a goat track to enjoy the splendid views from Dr Mary Booth Lookout. Or head west from the pool skirting pretty Lavender Bay, past Luna Park (now closed to the public), to the majestic Watt Park. Planted decades ago with bunya, Queensland kauri, Captain Cook, Norfolk Island and hoop pines, the park is a favourite among plant-lovers and makes a relaxing spot for a picnic. From the north shore you could catch a taxi back to the city via the the Sydney Harbour Tunnel (opened in 1992), but take another route if you suffer from claustrophobia.

Left: North Sydney Olympic Swimming Pool
Above: taking it easy

10. A PUB CRAWL *(see map, p55)*

The point of this itinerary is not inebriation, although that may be an occupational hazard. Drink light beer or lemon squash to maintain the regimen. A tour of these watering holes provides a glimpse into the lives of ordinary Australians, and into some of the social history that is woven into – or even formulated in – Sydney's pubs.

This pub crawl can start anytime after mid-morning, about the time when most of the city's pubs open. Begin at Sydney's beginnings… at **The Rocks**. There's a choice of three historical establishments: the **Lord Nelson Hotel** (corner of Kent and Argyle Streets; tel: 9251 4044), one of the oldest hotels in town, and now a bar, brasserie and brewery; the **Fortune of War Hotel** (137 George Street; tel: 9247 2714), which occupies the oldest hotel site in Sydney (it was built in 1922, replacing its 1839 namesake); and the **Hero of Waterloo** (81 Lower Fort Street; tel: 9252 4553), also a contender for the title of oldest pub. The Hero's cellars were reputedly used as holding cells for press-ganged sailors back in the 'roaring days'. All around are the Victorian-era houses of Lower Fort Street and the great wooden wharf sheds of Walsh Bay's Hickson Road.

Land of the Liquid Lunch

The colony of New South Wales was founded on rum, and by 1808 (the time of Governor William Bligh of the *Bounty* fame), it was the quasi-official currency of the colony. Today beer, 'the amber fluid', is Australia's favourite tipple – the country has been called 'land of the liquid lunch' – and an entire vocabulary has revolved around the drink. 'Tinnies' are tin cans, 'twisties' are twist-top bottles, 'stubbies' are also bottles. Fosters, Tooheys, Coopers, Castlemaine XXXX (pronounced 'Four Ex' – reputedly because Queenslanders can't spell 'beer') and Swan are some of the major brands, followed by the so-called 'boutique' beers like Hahn, Eumundi, Redback and Dogbolter

Above: a quiet drink at the Lord Nelson Hotel

etc. Also available, but more expensive, are imports like Heineken, NZ Steinlager, Corona, Guinness and others. Australian beers are served very cold in pubs and are generally higher in alcohol content than standard British or American brews. The 'middy', which costs around A$2 and up, is a manageable-sized beer of about half a pint, but drinking the larger 'schooner', around A$3 and up, is not going to get you through today's agenda if you sink one at each stop.

For a change of 'neck oil', try Queensland's Bundaberg rum, commonly called 'Bundy'. Australia produces excellent wines, served by the glass over the counter or available to buy by the bottle. 'House' wine by the glass will be the very *ordinaire* but 'Château Cardboard' (that is, from a boxed cask behind the bar counter) is passable. While Australian pub culture has historically been unmistakably male, all pubs have mixed drinking as a matter of law. It would be an inept publican who wasn't making some attempt to attract the ever-increasing number of financially independent professional women populating the city's workplaces.

Ersatz Oz

Meanwhile, back in **George Street** at The Rocks, move into the post-convict era at the Orient, Observer or Mercantile hotels. The re-gentrified **Orient** (corner of Argyle Street; tel: 9251 1255), a familiar after-work meeting place for office workers and professionals, serves good food. The more proletarian **Mercantile** (tel: 9217 6666) has a distinctly Irish flavour and features folk singers most nights – and Guinness-fuelled riotous times on St Patrick's Day or Melbourne Cup Day. The **Observer** (tel: 9252 4169) is equally welcoming and 'fair dinkum' Australian. In The Rocks' sea of ersatz Oz, the latter two places are sanctuaries for those Australians to whom 'duty-free' means a day off work, and who wouldn't be caught dead at the

'barbie' in a Ken Done apron. While in The Rocks, you may decide you never want to spend less that $10 on a drink again, in which case head for **Horizons** (tel: 9250 6000), the cigar-coloured top-floor bar of the **ANA Hotel** in Cumberland Street. And if you're still in the mood for views and expensive booze, trip up to the **Krug Room** (Level 41, Chifley Tower, Chifley Square; tel: 9221 2500), a genuine champagne bar with a profoundly luxurious setting.

Up in **Macquarie Street,** two hotels architecturally symbolise late 20th-century

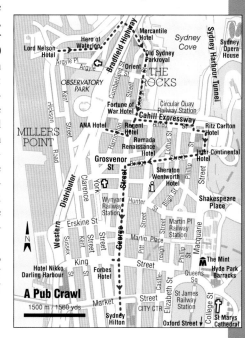

Sydney – by sticking it onto 19th-century buildings. Both of these five-star international chain hotels feature the nostalgia and elegant schizophrenia of architectural 'facade-ism'. The **Ritz-Carlton** (No 93; tel: 9252 4600) emerged from the bricks of a former VD clinic and hospital, while the much larger **Inter-Continental** (No 117; tel: 925 3900) sprouts from the shell of the once-lovely sandstone Colonial Treasury Building. In the former establishment, sink something like a stout or port in the clubby instant antiquity of the lobby bar. In the latter, tea in the central courtyard is quite genteel, but even whisky in the lounge bar on level 34 comes with a breathtaking view. The view stretches from the Sydney Domain, through the Harbour Heads and almost to New Zealand. The prices too are elevated, but with a vista like this the experience is a bargain.

A Yuppies' Hangout

Back down to earth, the **Forbes Hotel** (tel: 9299 3703) at the corner of York and King streets is another piece of renovated history, but without the high-rise implant. There's lots of polished wood, brass and stained glass in this colonial Central Business District boozer, which features both a pasta bar and grill. Today, it's a yuppies' hangout and a good place to rub shoulders with the after-office crowd.

A five-minute walk away in George Street (opposite the Queen Victoria Building), in the bowels of the Sydney Hilton Hotel, is the extraordinary Marble Bar (tel: 9266 2000). So precious a creation is this 1893 edifice that it was dismantled, then reassembled stone by stone when its original home, the George Adams Hotel, was removed in the early 1970s to make way for the Hilton. It is all green-marble, chintz, original paintings, stained glass and ornate columns – and an indicator of the great wealth that poured through Sydney in the 19th century. Lots of jazz and rock are played here.

As night closes in you can check out the gay pubs in **Oxford Street**, notably **The Exchange** (No 34; tel: 9331 1936), **Midnight Shift** (No 85; tel: 9360 4319) and, the **Albury** (No 6, tel: 9361 6555). They're flamboyant (and 'glamboyant'), and have raucous, camped-up entertainment. In Kings Cross, the **Celebrities Bar** in the **Sebel Townhouse** (23 Elizabeth Bay Road; tel: 9358 3244) is intimate and generally heterosexual. You might see some of the stars and entertainers who regularly patronise the hotel. The **Soho Bar** (171 Victoria Street; tel: 9358 6511) is younger and less formal (to get in, wear black, Darlinghurst's universal non-colour) and is a good example of Sydney pub deco architecture. To round the evening off, try a big meal at the sophisticated Asian noodle bar, the Wockpool (155 Victoria Street, Potts Point; tel: 9356 2911), which might help take the edge off tomorrow's hangover.

Above: a warm welcome at the Ritz-Carlton
Right: Botany Bay seen from Kurnell

11. BOTANY BAY *(see map, p58)*

Here's a chance to get out of the city, to cross the red-tiled suburbs and to arrive, yet again, at the ocean. It's perfect for a picnic at La Perouse or Kurnell. Combining wilderness, historical sites and a modern industrial 'frightscape', Botany Bay is where European Australia began…

You'll need a car for this tour. Starting at **Taylor Square** (in Oxford Street), drive south along ANZAC Parade. This long avenue passes a number of sacred sporting sites, the Sydney Football Stadium, the Sydney Cricket Ground, Moore Park Golf Course, Randwick Racecourse and the University of New South Wales. Nestled between the sporting venues is Rupert Murdoch's grand gift to Sydney – Fox Studios (tel: 9383 4000). Through Maroubra, continue south to **La Perouse** on the northern arm of Botany Bay. The 16-km (10-mile) drive from Sydney takes about 30 minutes.

Windswept **Botany Bay** is where European Australia began when, at 3pm on 29 April 1770, James Cook, RN, stepped ashore from the *Endeavour* to claim the 'Great South Land' for Britain. The place was named Botany Bay after more than 3,000 new botanical specimens were collected by the expedition's naturalist, Joseph Banks. Australia's most famous convict ballad, *Botany Bay*, was inspired by the place's fearful reputation. In 1788, the First Fleet anchored here briefly, found the site unsuitable for a permanent settlement, and moved to Sydney Cove.

Disappearance of the French

La Perouse Monument, built in 1828, marks the 1788 visit by a French fleet led by Comte de La Perouse, who arrived in Botany Bay six days after Captain Phillip and the First Fleet had left. After sailing from Botany Bay, La Perouse's ships disappeared off the face of the earth, or so it was thought until their wreckage was discovered in the Solomon Islands in 1828. The monument, the idea of Baron de Bougainville, who visited the site in 1825, is under the aegis of the NSW National Parks and Wildlife Service.

The 1882 **Old Cable Station** (Wed–Sun 10am–4.30pm; tel: 9311 3379) at ANZAC Parade, La Perouse, was built to house the workers operating the 1876 undersea telegraph line to New Zealand, and now houses the **La Per-**

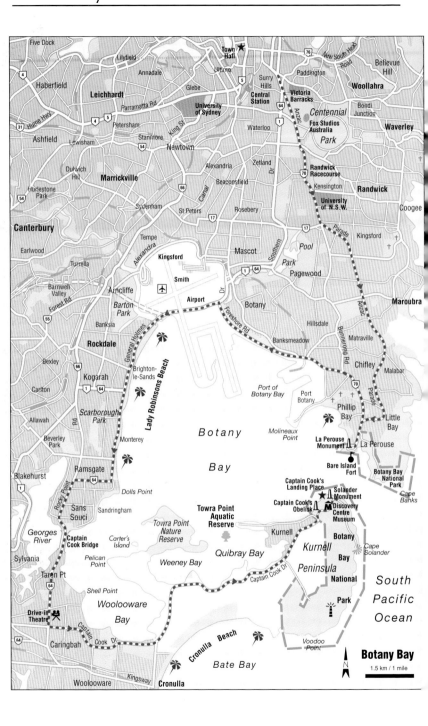

Five Dock
Lilyfield
Annadale
Haberfield
4
Leichhardt
Annandale
Ultimo
Glebe
Town Hall ★
New South Head Road
76
Paddington
Believue Hill
Woollahra
Parramatta Rd
University of Sydney
Surry Hills
Central Station
Victoria Barracks
64
Centennial Park
Fox Studios Australia
Bondi Junction
Waverley
31
Hume Hwy
Ashfield
Petersham
Stanmore
King St
Newtown
54
Lewisham
Dulwich Hill
Marrickville
Alexandria
Zetland
Waterloo
1
70
Randwick Racecourse
Kensington
University of N.S.W.
Randwick
Coogee
54
Hurlstone Park
66
Canal
Beaconsfield
Canterbury
Earlwood
St Peters
17
Roseberry
17
Kingsford
Maroubra
Turrella
Sydenham
Tempe
Southern
Pool
Park
Pagewood
Anzac
Barnwell Valley
Arncliffe
Kingsford
Smith
Mascot
1
64
Forest Rd
55
Barton Park
Airport ✈
Botany
Hillsdale
Banksmeadow
Matraville
Chifley
Malabar
Rockdale
Banksia
General Holmes Dr
Foreshore Rd
70
Bexley
66
Kogarah
Brighton-le-Sands
Port of Botany Bay
Port Botany
Phillip Bay
Little Bay
Carlton
1
64
Scarborough Park
Lady Robinsons Beach
Botany
Bay
Molineaux Point
La Perouse Monument
La Perouse
Allawah
Beverley Park
Monterey
Botany Bay National Park
Cape Banks
Blakehurst
Ramsgate
64
Dolls Point
Bare Island Fort
1
Rocky Point Rd
Sans Souci
Sandringham
Towra Point Aquatic Reserve
Captain Cook's Landing Place
Solander Monument
Discovery Centre Museum
Georges River
Captain Cook Bridge
Carter's Island
Towra Point Nature Reserve
Quibray Bay
Captain Cook's Obelisk
Botany
Cape Solander
Sylvania
Pelican Point
Weeney Bay
Kurnell
Kurnell Peninsula
Taren Pt
64
Shell Point
Captain Cook Dr
National
South
Pacific
Ocean
Drive-in Theatre
Wooloware Bay
Park
64
Caringbah
Captain Cook Dr
Cronulla Beach
Voodoo Point
Wooloware
Kingsway
Cronulla
Bate Bay
Botany Bay
1.5 km / 1 mile
N

ouse Museum. Nearby is the 1820s **Macquarie Watchtower**, the oldest building on the bay, erected by Governor Macquarie to tackle smugglers. Nearby lies the grave of Franciscan monk Père Receveur, who was a member of La Perouse's expedition. On Sunday afternoon this is a lively area, with local Aborigines, migrant families, picnickers and sightseers all enjoying the open space and fresh air. There is even a snake charmer's show (from 1.30pm) in the little metal enclosure near the last bus stop. Linked by a bridge to the shore is **Bare Island Fort**, constructed in 1881 in anticipation of French or Russian attacks, with barracks added in 1889. Enjoy a 45-minute tour on weekends (12.30–3.30pm; tel: 9311 3379).

The First European Footfall

On the southern arm of the bay, **Kurnell Peninsula**, the home of huge oil refineries, is the site of **Captain Cook's Landing Place**. Just 36km (22 miles) south of Sydney, it's a 20-minute drive from La Perouse along Foreshore Road, General Holmes Drive, the Grand Parade, Taren Point Road and Captain Cook Drive. Several monuments – the **Captain Cook Obelisk** (1870); **Sir Joseph Banks Memorial** (1947), **Solander Monument** (1914) and a memorial to **Seaman Forby Sutherland**, the first European known to be buried on the continent – mark the eight days Cook spent at Kurnell. The site is perfect for a quiet picnic, with views across the broad blue bay. A small offshore rock near the Obelisk is the site of the first recorded white footfall on eastern Australia – that of seaman Isaac Smith.

The National Parks and Wildlife Service maintains the **Banks-Solander Track** and the **Discovery Centre** museum (Mon–Fri 11am–3pm, Sat, Sun and public holidays, 10am–4.30pm; tel: 9668 9111). This part of the peninsula is good for easy bushwalks; the landscape is a mixture of open space, bush and rocky coastal fringes.

The Gwiyagal Aborigines who once inhabited this rich area would probably recognise the nearby **Towra Point Nature Reserve**, one of the city's last coastal wetland bird sanctuaries. (Entry is by National Parks and Wildlife Service permit; call the office, tel: 9668 9111, several days in advance.) Today a massive oil refinery occupies much of the interior of the peninsula. You can swim in the Botany Bay area, from La Perouse to any number of points along The Grand Parade to **Dolls Point**, right around to **Kurnell** – but remember to look out for sharks, especially in summer. Look for the meshed enclosures. You might continue south to **Cronulla**, the city's southernmost and longest surf beach with 10km (6 miles) of sand dunes stretching south from Kurnell.

ANCHORING THE 'ENDEAVOUR'
In front of you out on the bay, approximately 500 metres away, there is a red buoy. This is the site where Captain James Cook anchored the 'Endeavour' in 1770.

The Maritime Services Board now maintains this site as one of its navigational markers for ships entering Botany Bay.

Right: Captain Cook's Landing Place at Kurnell

Excursions

EXCURSION 1. BLUE MOUNTAINS *(see map, p62)*

Although some of the attractions of the Blue Mountains can be visited by a combination of rail and taxi, the best way to explore this area is by car. You could spend up to a week in the mountains, but a full day will give you a taste of what the area has to offer.

Seen from any Sydney vantage point, the thin line of the Blue Mountains on the western horizon looks unimpressive. The mountains are not very high; **Mount Victoria**, on the Great Western Highway is, at a mere 1,111 metres (3,645ft), the highest – and coldest – point in the range. However, this plateau is so deeply indented that it took 24 years for the first white settlers to find a way across the mountains to the pasture lands of the west. Most of the walks in this unusual mountain terrain involve heading down from the road then back up to the car at the end of the day.

The Blue Mountains get their name from a trick of the light. When viewed from a distance, refracted light on droplets of eucalyptus oil in the atmosphere – from the millions of gum trees on the mountains – creates a blue haze. Popular with bushwalkers and rock climbers on account of its grand vistas and beautiful gorges and valleys, the area is part of one of NSW's largest national parks. When it's hot in Sydney, the mountain glens are pleasantly cool, but in winter, the cool temperatures, log fires and the occasional snowfall create a striking contrast to Sydney's temperate days.

Forest Trails

In the 1870s, the Blue Mountains were regarded primarily as a holiday centre for Sydneysiders – a role they retained for several decades. But by the 1970s, the mountains had fallen out of favour. Since then, the area has gone through a renaissance of sorts, and to-day, there are new resorts, some highly regarded restaurants, and eucalyptus forest trails full of healthy walkers.

Katoomba, 100km (62 miles) west of Sydney, is the major tourist centre of the Blue Mountains and has been a holiday resort for more than a century. Built on a series of hills that drop steeply into the **Jamison Valley**, the town is served by electric trains from Sydney (some 90 minutes away) and is on the Great Western Highway. To orientate yourself, head for the tourist information centre at

Left: walking in the Blue Mountains
Right: the Blue Mountains' natural beauty

Echo Point (daily, 9am–5pm; tel: 4739 6266). A short trail leads to the point that provides a magnificent view past the famous **Three Sisters** rock formation over Jamison Valley.

The nearby **Giants Stairway** descends 1,000 steps to the valley floor, from which there are walks of varying length and difficulty. Treks to the **Ruined Castle** and **Mount Solitary** from here will take most of the day, are fairly hard and require planning. Details of these and other walks are available from the Blue Mountains Visitor Information Centres at Glenbrook (daily 8.30am–5pm; tel: 4739 6266), on the Great Western Highway and at Echo Point (daily 9am–5pm), and the National Parks and Wildlife Service Heritage Centre at Govetts Leap Road, Blackheath (daily 9am–4.30pm; tel: 4787 8877).

One of the easiest walks from the bottom of the stairway is to the right towards the base of the **Scenic Railway** (daily 9am–5pm; tel: 4782 2699). This enduring tourist attraction, which has operated safely for many years, was originally constructed in the 1880s to transport miners and coal up from the valley. This is a good point to bear in mind as you ascend a sheer cliff face on a seemingly flimsy contraption. Going down is even worse: one has the terrifying sensation of plunging 445 metres (1,460ft) to the valley floor (in fact it's a 45° incline).

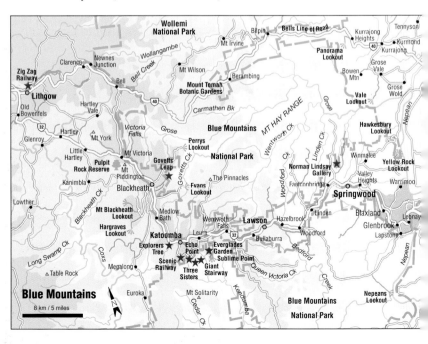

excursions

Leura, one of the prettiest villages in the mountains, adjoins Katoomba and is reached by a scenic clifftop drive. Its historic main street is full of craft, antiques and tea shops. **Everglades Gardens** (daily 10am–5pm; 37 Everglades Avenue; tel: 4784 1938), features 5 hectares (12 acres) of landscaped grounds. The stately home **Leuralla** (daily 10am–5pm; Olypian Parade; tel: 4784 1169), once the residence of the UN's first president, Dr HV Evatt, includes a collection of 19th-century art and a restaurant. Call in at the luxurious **Fairmont Resort** (Sublime Point Road; tel: 4782 5222) poised on the clifftop at Sublime Point, just outside of town.

The other up-market resort in the mountains is **Lilianfels** at Echo Point (tel: 4780 1200), near Katoomba. The 85-room country retreat, built around a historic 1890 home, features a large ornamental garden, bushwalking tracks, fine views of the Jamison Valley and a good restaurant. There's a variety of cheap accommodation throughout the Blue Mountains.

An Edwardian Folly

Continuing on the highway along the ridge westwards from Katoomba, the road passes the Explorers Tree, which marks the crossing of this seemingly impenetrable range by explorers Gregory Blaxland, William Lawson and William Wentworth in 1813. For the very adventurous, this is also the starting point for the 42-km (25-mile) Six Foot Track, a bushwalk that takes two to three days and ends at Jenolan Caves. Further on, stop at the **Hydro Majestic Hotel** at Medlow Bath (tel: 4788 1002). Built between 1880 and 1903, this extraordinary hotel is an Edwardian folly with art deco touches and a cavernous dining room with stunning views over the Megalong Valley.

Blackheath is the next main town along the highway. Originally called Hounslow, the settlement was renamed by Macquarie upon his return from Bathurst in 1815 because of its black, wild look. The town was a favourite stopping place for 19th-century miners heading west to dig for gold.

The **Bacchante Gardens** (daily, 10am–4pm; Bacchante Street; tel: 4787 7624) features more than 1,500 rhododendrons in a bush setting, and is well worth a visit, especially in the spring (Sept–Nov). The area has spectacular views of the tree-lined Grose Valley from **Evans Lookout** and **Govetts Leap**, which are starting points for several bushwalks into the national park. The best introduction to the mountains is the **Grand Canyon walk**, a three- or four-hour, fairly easy hike. Take the signposted road out to

Above left: Three Sisters, Katoomba
Right: a Blue Mountains garden in spring

Evans Lookout, where you leave the car, and descend a fairly steep trail into the rainforest and canyon. The canyon itself is a narrow passage lined with ferns. Climb through a sunny, shaded glen to return to the road.

The only hard part of the walk from **Perry's Lookdown** to the **Blue Gum Forest** is the descent to the valley floor and the climb at the end of the day (to Perry's Lookdown or Govetts Leap). The Blue Gum Forest, with its crystal-clear streams, grassy swathes and towering eucalyptus trees is an ideal goal for a day's walk. As with all of the longer walks, you should drop in at the Heritage Centre (*see above*) to inform park staff of your planned route.

On Horseback

From Blackheath, you can drive down from the escarpment on the other side into the Megalong Valley, a tranquil farming area that offers horse-riding excursions at the Megalong Valley Australian Heritage Centre (tel: 4787 8188) or Werriberri Trail Rides (tel: 4787 9171). On the way back to the city, stop at the **Norman Lindsay Gallery and Museum** (daily 10am–4pm; tel: 4751 1067) at Faulconbridge. Lindsay was one of Australia's most acclaimed (and notorious) painters, and also a writer and sculptor. He lived in this stone house for 57 years up to his death in 1969. The house, and its paintings, drawings, novels and ship models, is owned by the National Trust. The gardens include some of Lindsay's larger statues and fountains, and his studio, set up as if in readiness for his reappearance. Also along Macquarie

---

Jenolan Caves

If you have more than a day to spare in the mountains, a turn-off from the Great Western Highway just outside Hartley (130km/81 miles from Sydney), will take you the 48km (30 miles) to **Jenolan Caves**, renowned as Australia's most famous limestone cave system.

After passing through Hampton State Forest, you skirt the Kanangra Boyd National Park along a steep, winding road and eventually round a bend to be confronted by the surprising spectacle of the 24-metre (79-ft) high **Grand Arch**. The road turns into this gaping cleft in the hillside and emerges outside the Tudor-style sandstone **Jenolan Caves House** (tel: 6359 3322). Built at the turn of the century, Jenolan Caves House has attracted visitors since the caves were first opened to the public. Like much of the mountain facilities, it was looking seedy until a few years ago when new management renovated it to a high standard of comfort.

According to legend, the caves were first discovered by white settlers during the pursuit of a bushranger in 1838. Almost 30 years later they were opened to the public, and now six cavern systems are open. These caverns contain an astounding diversity of formations – stalactites, stalagmites, paper-thin 'straws' and other strangely contorted shapes – all created by the action of air on dripping, limestone-bearing water. The entire cave system forms a massive underground labyrinth. Some of the caves can be explored without a guide, others may only be visited as part of a regular tour. For information, phone the Jenolan Caves Trust Reserve (tel: 6359 3311). Wear sound walking shoes with a good grip and be prepared for quite a lot of climbing up and down steps.

excursions

Parade in Faulconbridge is the **Prime Ministers' Corridor of Oaks**, in which every Australian prime minister or his family has planted a tree.

Another way back to Sydney is via the northern route along the Bell's Line of Road. Rail buffs might take a detour via Lithgow, an industrial town set in a narrow valley on the western side of the range. Coal has been mined here since 1869 and new mines and a power station have grown around the 19th-century buildings in the town's main street. The **Zig Zag Railway** (tel: 6351 4826), a 13-km (8-mile) section of tracks built in the 1860s to descend the western escarpment of the mountains, is just a few kilometres before Lithgow. Rail enthusiasts operate the steam-train line (Mon–Fri 11am, 1pm and 3pm, Sat and Sun 10.30am, 12.15pm, 2pm and 3.30pm). Trains leave from Clarence Station, between Bell and Lithgow; fares range from $13 for adults and $6 for children.

If you head east towards Sydney, you will find the tiny historic village of **Mount Wilson**. Settled as a holiday resort for the wealthy in the late 19th century, its quiet lanes remains virtually unchanged. It has acres of superb gardens, many of which are open to the public. For information call the Blue Mountains Visitor Information Centre (tel: 4739 6266).

A little further on, **Mount Tomah Botanic Garden** (Bells Line of Road, via Bilpin; open daily 10am–5pm; tel: 4567 2154) is the cool-climate cousin of the Royal Botanic Gardens. Highlights include the rhododendron collection and the Formal Garden. The Botanic Gardens are terraced down the side of Mount Tomah and the views are sensational. Mount Tomah boasts one of the country's best out-of-town restaurants. Call first (tel: 4567 2060).

EXCURSION 2. NORTHERN BEACHES
AND THE HAWKESBURY *(see map, p66)*

The Northern Beaches and the Hawkesbury are really two different trips. Although they are close geographically, Broken Bay – at the mouth of the Hawkesbury – and Pittwater separate the access routes. You can, however, do a quick run up to the northern beaches, board a ferry at Palm Beach, and slip across Pittwater for bit of an introductory tour of Ku-ring-gai. Or you can skip the drive up the northern beaches and head straight for the Hawkesbury *(see box on page 68)*.

From the city, cross the Harbour Bridge and drive along Military Road through the boutique shopping strip of Neutral Bay, Cremorne and Mosman. After the Spit Bridge you have a choice: either turn right into Sydney Road to Manly, or follow the signs to Dee Why. (Manly is covered in the Sydney Harbour Cruises, *page 31* and The Spit to Manly Harbour Walk, *page 49* itineraries) If you take the Manly road, drive along the ocean beach to Queenscliff, then over the headland to **Harboard**. This narrow, gently sloping beach has one of Sydney's safest surfs, and can therefore be recommended to beginners and families. (Bear in mind that you should never swim at an unpatrolled beach in Australia. Most

Above left: Jenolan Caves
Right: ready to surf

Sydney beaches are patrolled by lifeguards from October to April, generally on weekends and during school holidays. And don't forget to swim between the flags.) Follow the coast road to Curl Curl and Dee Why beach. Turn left on Dee Why Parade and then right when you come to Pittwater Road.

Passing **Dee Why Lagoon**, now a nature reserve, on your right, you come to **Long Reef**, where one of the world most scenic – and treeless – golf courses takes up the whole headland. Turn right into ANZAC Avenue at the end of the golf course and drive up to the lookout. From here you gaze upon a land where it is always afternoon, a vista of purple-green headlands and golden beaches fringed with foaming surf, set against a sea of deepest blue and an endless summer sky.

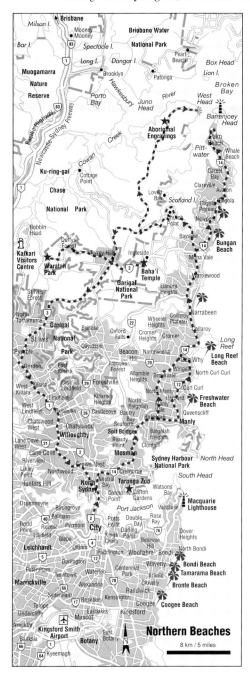

Clean Surf

Leaving Long Reef, you pass Collaroy beach and come to **Narrabeen**, where the large lagoon is a favourite with water-skiers. At the Mona Vale shopping centre, turn right into Barrenjoey Road and climb the headland overlooking **Newport Beach**. Turn right at Karlo Parade, right into Bungan Road and park on the corner of Myola Road. A long steep hill descends on your right to **Bungen Beach**, Sydney's most secluded and undeveloped beach which, on weekdays, is shared by just a handful of surfers. Remember to bring your own refreshments.

Leave Bungan Beach by Bungan Head Road, crossing Barrenjoey Road into Beaconsfield Street, which will bring you to the legendary Newport Arms in Kalinya Street (tel: 9997 4900) on a

back reach of Pittwater. Lunch and a few drinks in the beer garden will give you the opportunity to observe those lotus-eaters fortunate enough to inhabit this exotic paradise known as the Pittwater Peninsula.

Climbing up from Newport, turn right off the Barrenjoey Road at The Serpentine. **Bilgola Beach** is in a small, sub-tropical rainforest of ferns and exotic blooms set deep into the plateau between high headlands. Bilgola is one of Sydney's smallest and best beaches. A kiosk supplies basic refreshments.

Avalon, the last major shopping centre on the Pittwater Pensinula, has plenty of coffee bars and restaurants. After Avalon, turn right off Pittwater Road onto Whale Beach Road, which wends its way to **Whale Beach**. The drive over the headland offers breathtaking views over **Palm Beach**, **Barrenjoey** and **Broken Bay**. Should you wish to pause to enjoy the view, book a table at Jonahs (69 Bynya Road, Palm Beach; tel: 9974 5599), where you can stay the night. Near Palm Beach, just opposite the golf course, is the Beach Road Restaurant (1 Beach Road, Palm Beach; tel: 9947 1159), which serves some of the city's best food in a sub-tropical garden setting. Both the beach and peninsula side of Palm Beach have a range of cafés and fish-and-chip joints. If you are energetic, walk along Palm Beach to Barrenjoey Lighthouse, perched 113 metres (371ft) above Broken Bay at the tip of the peninsula.

The Basin

From a jetty on the Pittwater side of Palm Beach you can hop on a ferry operated by the Palm Beach Ferry Service (tel: 9974 5235) for a cruise of Pittwater and Broken Bay. Passengers can alight at West Head where there is a walking track leading to the Aboriginal art at an area known as The Basin, in the **Ku-ring-gai Chase National Park**. The Basin's collection, probably the most extensive example of indigenous art in the Sydney area, was created by the Gurringai people who occupied this beautiful territory for more than 20,000 years. The same area can be explored by road on your way home from Palm Beach. Turn right into Pittwater Road from Barrenjoey Road and continue to West Head Road. This will give you access to both the art site and, fur-

bove: northern beaches panorama
ight: heels over head

ther on, the tip of West Head, often called one of the best coastal views in the world. On your return journey, turn right at Mona Vale Road and head west up the plateau to the exotic **Baha'i Temple** (daily, 9am–5pm; 173 Mona Vale Road; tel: 9913 8063). The temple honours what adherents describe as an all-encompassing world religion that respects belief in the Buddha, Mohammed and Jesus Christ, among others.

Further west along Mona Vale Road, you can take the Booralie Road turn-off (right) to get to **Waratah Park and Animal Sanctuary** (daily 10am–5pm; Namba Road, Duffys Forest; tel: 9450 2377). This sanctuary is home to a selection of various native animals within a 30-hectare (74-acre) bushland setting, and offers picnic facilities and suchlike, but its major claim to international fame is that it was formerly the residence of Skippy the Bush Kangaroo. Skippy starred in the 1960s television series of the same name, and remains probably the greatest-ever ambassador for his species.

Sydney direct to the Hawkesbury

Pick up the Warringah Freeway from the northern side of the Harbour Bridge, and turn onto the Pacific Highway, heading north through a long band of well-established leafy suburbs. Turn right onto Bobbin Head Road, which takes you to the heart of Ku-ring-gai Chase National Park. This area, with its sandstone outcrops, sparkling waterways, and rugged bush, is an impressive example of biodiversity (there are some 1,000 plant species) and its stunning natural beauty is said to represent pre-colonial Sydney. First stop should be the Bobbin Head Information Centre (daily 10am–4pm; Ku-ring-gai Chase Road, Cowan Creek; tel: 9472 8949), where you can pick up information on walks and other activities. If you have time, continue north (leave the park via Ku-ring-gai Chase Road and turn right on the Pacific Highway). Not far away is Brooklyn, where you'll find the Hawkesbury Riverboat Postman (tel: 9985 7566), the last river postal service in Australia. You can hop aboard for the four-hour post run, but you will have be on deck by 9.30am. Brooklyn is a large boating centre – you can bob around in a dinghy or take a week's holiday aboard a self-drive luxury houseboat. For information call the Hawkesbury River Tourist Information Centre (tel: 9985 7064). If you don't have a car, come by train from Central Station. Call transport information (tel: 131500) for further details.

Above: Hawkesbury River Bridge

EXCURSION 3. SYDNEY'S WEST *(see map, p18–19 and 70)*

The introduction of a ferry service along the Parramatta River and the building of a new freeway, the M4, have provided good access to the attractions of the west, including the historic sites of Parramatta, the wildlife sanctuaries and the shining new centrepiece – Olympic Park.

If you're planning to drive, you should head for Broadway (the extension of George Street), which will take you on to the M4. But a better option is to take the RiverCat from Circular Quay and glide in comfort past the interesting sites west of the bridge (ring transport information, tel: 131500, for times of departures). If you have time, hop off at the Homebush Bay Ferry Wharf for a tour of Olympic Park (tours are not operating during the Olympics). Olympic Explorer Buses leave from the wharf, as well as the railway station, and whisk passengers off for a peek at some of the best sporting facilities in the world, at least until the next Olympics are staged. For further information on exploring the area, ring the Homebush Bay Visitor Information Centre (daily, except during the Olympics; 1 Herb Elliot Avenue; tel: 9714 7888).

Symbolic Heartland

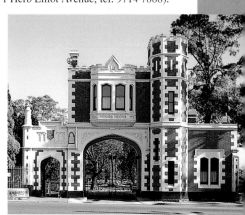

Parramatta, 53 minutes from the city by water, is the symbolic heartland of the west, although an expanding population has pushed the geographical centre further out. It is also Australia's second-oldest settlement. Members of the First Fleet established the area after discovering that the soil along the shores of Sydney Harbour was inadequate for the cultivation of European crops. The rich river flats of Parramatta, easily reached by boat, provided a good solution. Today the area lays claim to some of Australia's oldest and most interesting historic sites. Start your tour at the **Parramatta Visitors' Centre** (daily; tel: 9630 3703), just 10 minutes from the wharf, where you can pick up maps and general information on the area. The attractions are a walk or a short bus ride away from the centre.

Located in Parramatta Park, **Old Government House** (Mon–Fri 10am–4pm, Sat and Sun 11am–4pm; tel: 9635 8149) was built in 1799 and is said to be Australia's oldest public building. The importance of the settlement to the colony can be seen in the fact that various governors settled here, rather than in Sydney Cove. The building is pleasant but not grand. Its simple Georgian style would have been suitable for only minor gentry back in England – the settlers weren't interested in putting on a big show in what was, after all, just a penal colony. **Elizabeth Farm** (daily 10am–5pm; tel: 9365 9488) in Alice Street, Rosehill (next door to Parramatta) was built in 1793, and is Australia's oldest surviving building. Its generous verandas and relaxed atmosphere anticipate the development of the ubiquitous homestead style of housing. It was

bove: the entrance to Parramatta Park

Olympic Games

The Sydney 2000 Olympic Games is the biggest event ever held in Australia and the first major world event of the millennium. Some 10,000 athletes from 200 countries, 5,000 officials, 1,500 members of the media and millions of visitors are descending on the city for the Games (15 Sept–1 Oct; Paralympics 18–29 Oct). Since winning the right to stage the event in 1993, when it could barely boast a decent Olympic-sized swimming pool, the city has been in a frenzy of development. Now it can claim sporting facilities second to none, including a pool said to be the world's 'fastest'.

The industrial site of Homebush Bay has been transformed into Olympic Park, incorporating 600 hectares (nearly 1,500 acres) of new parkland and a grand boulevard built on a Napoleonic scale. Sydney has been busy scrubbing, scraping and polishing; roads have been fixed, decade-old public transport problems have been solved, abandoned buildings have been refurbished and there's public art all over the place.

Tickets to Olympic events went on sale a year before the games, so chances of getting into events, if you haven't already booked, are rather slim. But you might have some luck with cancellations, or with the less popular sports. Finding accommodation presents similar challenges.

Although Olympic Park is the main venue, a number of other sites in town are hosting a variety of events. The triathlon runs across the Opera House precinct while sailing takes place around Sydney Harbour; both are partially non-ticket events, which means free public access. Other sports free for spectators include the marathon, racewalk and road cycling. There's beach volleyball at Bondi Beach, a variety of indoor sports at Darling Harbour venues and football at Centennial Parklands, as well as at interstate venues.

The Sydney 2000 Olympic Arts Festival (18 Aug–30 Sept) is another triumph of statistics: some 4,000 artists appearing in 400 performances of 53 productions, plus 50 visual exhibitions at 29 venues. Although the big events at the arts festival will be pre-sold, tickets to smaller performances are available, as is entrance to the visual exhibitions, whose highlights include the Dead Sea Scrolls on display at the Art Gallery and a Leonardo da Vinci manuscript, on loan from Bill Gates, at the Powerhouse.

Travel to events is by public transport, on which ticket holders to the games and arts festival can travel free. The Sydney 2000 Games Information Service (tel: 136363) and the official website (www.olympics.com) have details about the Olympics and the arts festival. Ray White Real Estate (tel: 9262 3700; website: www-raywhite.com.au) has details of homestay accommodation (private rentals).

Sydney Olympic Park

1000 m / 1100 yds

excursions

built as the home of John and Elizabeth Macarthur, who occupied the top rung of the colony's pastoral elite for years. He served in the colonial government before leading the Rum Rebellion against Governor Bligh in 1808; she looked after the farm. Her sheep-breeding programme started what would become one of the country's most important industries. There are a few interesting sites in the vicinity of both these places; ask staff for directions.

The Biggest Theme Park

Those with a penchant for wildlife can continue from here. To visit **Wonderland Sydney** (daily 10am–5pm; Wallgrove Road, Eastern Creek; tel: 9830 9100), take a train from Parramatta Station to Rooty Hill. This is Australia's biggest theme park and, in addition to wild rides, an artificial beach and daily shows featuring sheep dogs, shearing and whip-cracking, the complex has a great native-wildlife park. See a 5-metre (16-ft) saltie (saltwater crocodile) and plenty of cuddly marsupials – koalas, kangaroos and wombats. Buses run between the complex and Rooty Hill Station.

The alternative to Wonderland Sydney is a trip to **Featherdale Wildlife Park** in Doonside (daily 10am–5pm; Kildare Road; tel: 9622 1644). Take the train from Parramatta to Doonside Station (then walk for 15 minutes to the sanctuary), or to Blacktown Station, and board a bus. Featherdale is a well-run centre featuring Australian species in natural enclosures. Facilities include a café and picnic areas.

Finish the day with a meal and stroll in one of the ethnic areas of west Sydney. **Little Italy** in Leichhardt is an easy trip by car, but those on public transport will have to return to the city to pick up a 438 bus from Circular Quay. This is one of the oldest of Sydney's multicultural communities. Head for Norton Street, where you'll find trattorias, pizzerias and gelatarias, and the best coffee in the city. Little Saigon, based around John Street, Cabramatta (a quick train ride from Parramatta) is the heartland of Sydney's large Vietnamese community. It has an intensely Asian feel to it, unlike the more westernised environment of Chinatown in the city centre This is a living, working community, not a place that people just visit for a meal – although there's plenty of that going on as well. Do some shopping, stop for a superb cheap meal or walk along the bustling streets before you return to Sydney.

Above: Wonderland Sydney, the country's biggest theme park
Right: a taste of Little Italy

EXCURSION 4. ROYAL NATIONAL PARK *(see map, below)*

The Royal National Park at Sutherland is the second-oldest national park in the world. While it may lack a sense of real outback wilderness, it has the decided advantage of being the city's most accessible bushland.

The **Royal National Park** at Sutherland, on the southern boundary of Sydney, had a historical role of global significance. It was created in 1879 and is the second-oldest public reserve in the world – only Yellowstone in the US (formed in 1872) is older. But the Royal was the world's first 'national park'. The Sydney park became 'Royal' to honour a visit by Queen Elizabeth in 1954. With the establishment of this park, the concept of natural areas set aside for public use was born. Yet the park's founders didn't care about native bush – the park was intended as a pleasure ground modelled after London's Hampstead Heath. Australian bush was replaced by imported plants and manicured lawns. Until 1922, the trust for this 15,000 hectare (37,065-acre) area earned an income from logging. Rabbits and foxes were introduced, and Javanese rusa deer and fallow deer, first released in the park in the late 1890s, are still there.

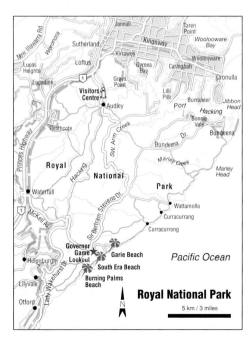

Royal National Park

5 km / 3 miles

Above: Royal National Park

excursions

Birds of a Feather

Although the park lacks a feeling of wilderness in the most popular locations, several areas of attractive bushland can be found if you're prepared to walk. Bounded by Port Hacking to the north, the Pacific Ocean to the east and the railway line to the west, the park is predominantly a heath-covered sandstone plateau. The valleys contain pockets of rainforest, with a luminous green luxuriance of buttress roots, liana vines and innumerable ferns. The native animals are timid and most are nocturnal so they're not nearly as visible as the 200 species of birds that inhabit the park. Within the park's dense grottoes you may hear a whip bird (its call sounds like a stock whip being cracked) or see the exquisite lyre bird, named after its lyre-shaped tail. Look out for the satin bower bird: it resembles a raven at first glance but a closer look reveals its plumage to be a deep, iridescent mauve.

The park is easy to reach from Sydney by road or public transport. If you have a car, follow the Princes Highway for about 45 minutes to the turn-off into the park at **Loftus**. If you are travelling by train, take the Illawarra line and disembark at one of the several stations around or within the park (Waterfall, Helensburg or Otford), then walk in. Or you can take a train to Cronulla, followed by a ferry across Port Hacking to **Bundeena** (book in advance during holiday periods, tel: 9523 2990). The main visitor centre and wildlife shop (daily 8.30am–4.30pm; tel: 9542 0648) is at **Audley**, where there is lots of information about the park. For information in advance call the **National Parks and Wildlife Service** information line on 1300 36 1967. There are over 150km (90 miles) of walking trails and numerous picnic and barbecue facilities within the park. You can rent canoes and paddleboats at Audley.

The roads through the park are not merely local-access routes: several are through roads between the south coast and Sydney (the Princes Highway to Wollongong skirts the park's western boundary), and the Bundeena Road is the only street that leads to the fishing village of Bundeena. **Lady Carrington Drive**, following the Hacking River valley, is flat and wide, and closed to traffic, so it's good for both cycling and walking.

Along the shores of the park are 21km (13 miles) of coastline; surfing beaches interspersed by rugged sandstone headlands. The beaches at **Era, Burning Palms** and **Garie** are the most popular surfing beaches and **Bundeena** is a renowned windsurfing area. The well-appointed camping area of **Bonnie Vale** nearby is adjacent to a sandy spot that is good for swimming. If you want to enjoy this facility, it is essential to book beforehand; during busy periods contact the park (tel: 9542 0648) several months in advance. The lagoon at **Wattamolla** is excellent for swimming, and is especially attractive to snorkellers and divers.

Right: sun, sand and sea

Leisure Activities

SHOPPING

There's much more to shopping in Sydney than opals and boomerangs. The shopping ideas on the next few pages cover many tastes, but stop short of that favourite export of many Asian tourists – freezer packs of prime Aussie beef. The only limits are your budget and the inevitable excess-baggage allowance.

Retail trading hours in Sydney are generally from 9am–5.30pm on weekdays, except on Thursday evenings when shopping hours extend till 9pm. Most major department stores and a good selection of smaller speciality shops are open Saturdays and Sundays 10am to 4pm. The Harbourside Shopping Centre at Darling Harbour (tel: 9281 3999) is open until 9pm every night. Some bookshops (such as Ariel at 42 Oxford Street, Paddington; tel: 9332 4581) are open till late, and sometimes all weekend. Chinatown shops are open daily from 8.30am to at least 6pm.

If you discover a purchase to be faulty, take it back for an exchange or refund (always hold on to your receipts). New South Wales has clear consumer-protection laws. If you then experience difficulties with the vendor, call the Department of Fair Trading (tel: 133220).

Australiana

'Australiana' covers a multitude of sins and kins. Americans (who have enough beef at home) tend to stock up on Akubra felt hats and Driza Bone oilskin coats for the 'Man from Snowy River' look. Many stores stock Australian rural gear, but the most famous one is **R M Williams** (389 George Street and elsewhere; tel: 9262 2228), because the old living legend, 'R.M.' himself, designed, wears and still manufactures much of it. **Thomas Cook Boot & Clothing** (790 George Street; tel: 9212 6616) carries a large range of high-country gear. Less macho garments can be found at various **Ken Done** shops (Sydney Airport, QVB, The Rocks and

Bondi Beach; tel: 9251 6099). Done is an Australian designer whose ubiquitous work is very wearable. For sheepskin products, try The Sheepskin Shop (139 George Street, The Rocks; tel: 9241 1099).

The **Australian Museum** (corner of William and College streets; tel: 9320 6150), **Museum of Sydney** (37 Phillip Street; tel: 9251 5988) and **State Library of New South Wales** (Macquarie Street; tel: 9231 1611) all have shops that carry an excellent range of books and other items with Australian themes.

Sydney has good outdoor markets selling everything from designer fashion to second-hand chic. Try the Balmain Markets (Sat from 7.30am on Darling Street in the grounds of St Andrews, Balmain; tel: 9818 2674), Glebe Markets (Sat 9am–4pm; in Glebe public school grounds; tel: 4237 7499) and Paddy's Markets (weekends 9am–4.30pm in Haymarket, near Chinatown; tel: 1300 361 589). If you've worked up an appetite, visit the Sydney Fish Markets at Pyrmont to view the daily catch and eat at one of the many restaurants in Waterfront Arcade.

Sydney's most popular market is the **Paddington Village Bazaar**, held on Saturdays in the Uniting Church in Oxford Street (tel: 9331 2646). Products include home-made jam, clothes by young fashion designers, jewellery, art and sculpture, second-hand clothes, books and other collectibles.

Popular tourist shopping beats are **The Rocks**, **Chinatown**, **Darling Harbour** (Harbourside Shopping Centre) and **Birken-**

Left: the Queen Victoria Building
Right: quintessential Australia

head Point (at Drummoyne). The Central Business District area bounded by Hunter, Park, Clarence and Elizabeth streets is popular for retail and duty-free shopping. It contains, among others, **Centrepoint** (tel: 9231 1000), the **Imperial Arcade** (tel: 9233 5662), **Mid-City Complex** (tel: 9221 2422), **Strand Arcade** (tel: 9232 4199), **Skygarden** (tel: 9231 1811) and **Queen Victoria Building** (tel: 9264 9209). These all house scores of speciality gift, clothing, book, music, jewellery and craft and art shops.

Beyond the city area, the suburbs renowned for power purchasing include **Mosman**, **Neutral Bay** and **Chatswood** (all north of the Bridge) and **Paddington**, **Bondi Junction** and **Double Bay** to the east of the city. **Gowings** (on the corner of George and Market streets, city; tel: 9264 6321, and 82 Oxford Street, Dorlinghurst; tel: 9331 5544) specialises in quality gifts, clothing and outdoor equipment. **Sax Leather** (110A Oxford Street; tel: 9331 6105) has very good sandals and belts.

At the **Golden Square** corner of King, Castlereagh and Elizabeth streets top international design houses hawk their wares in elegant surroundings. Nearby, Sydney's favourite department store, **David Jones** (known as DJs), is billed as 'the most beautiful store in the world'. There are two DJs in Sydney, one on Elizabeth Street and one on Market Street (tel: 9266 5544), the former the more elegant of the two but the latter with a basement food hall filled with scrumptious offerings.

Opals

Many jewellery shops in the central shopping district (particularly in Pitt and Castlereagh streets) sell Australian opals and sapphires, either set or loose. Look for 'black' opals (nearly always sold as a thin wafer of opal between a dark backing and a transparent cap) and 'white' opals (a light background shot through with colours, normally sold as a solid stone). Good opals aren't cheap, and there's lots of competition, so shop around.

Aboriginal Art

Bark paintings are the most common form of Koori (Aboriginal) art, but look out for contemporary works on board, boomerangs and didgeridoos. Prices for paintings can start at A$100. Try the **Hogarth Galleries**, 7 Walker Lane, Paddington (tel: 9360 6839), the **Aboriginal and Tribal Art Centre**, 1/117 George Street, the Rocks (tel: 9241 5998) or **Coo-ee Aboriginal Art Gallery** (98 Oxford Street; tel: 9332 1544), which stocks wonderful Aboriginal arts and crafts.

Food

Local delicacies include macadamia nuts, bush honey, royal jelly, chocolates and the inevitable Vegemite, a savoury spread. The **David Jones Food Hall** downstairs in the Market Street store (tel: 9266 5544) carries a good range. Australian wines can be purchased at any pub or bottle shop, with fair quality wines starting at A$10 per bottle. The standard-bearer of Australian (red) wines is Penfolds Grange Hermitage.

EATING OUT

In range, quality and value, Sydney has some of the best dining in the world. Successive waves of immigrants have introduced many different national styles of cooking. Few countries can match the diversity and quality of Australia's natural produce, particularly seafood, and Sydney's harbour and beaches offer unrivalled settings and views. There are no service charges, and the Australian dollar's low value against major currencies makes even Sydney's most expensive restaurants accessible to far more people than their counterparts in New York, Paris or London.

Many restaurants offer 'modern Australian cuisine'. This has resulted from a fusion of the world's various culinary traditions, particularly French, Italian, Thai, Chinese and Japanese. Modern Australian restaurants usually lean towards one particular ethnic tradition, while ethnic restaurants often adapt the ingredients and techniques of the modern Australian chefs to traditional recipes. The terms 'modern Australian' and 'ethnic' usually reflect the emphasis the chef places on particular ingredients and techniques.

Restaurant wine lists should be approached with caution. A shortage of premium Australian reds is pushing up prices. If you are not certain what to expect you should order by the glass; choose riesling and sémillon in preference to chardonnay, and perhaps one of the lighter, more commercial reds in preference to an underage Coonawarra cabernet or Hunter shiraz. You can save money by dining at BYO (bring your own) restaurants, even though they usually charge a small amount for corkage. Asian restaurants can be good value because, although most offer basic wine lists, the food tends to be better suited to beer or tea.

Sydney's hundreds of restaurants and cafés offer visitors a vast array of choices. Serious diners should consult the latest editions of the following publications – available at most newsagents and book stores for under $20 – for more detailed information: *The Sydney Morning Herald Good Food Guide; Cheap Eats; Sydney*

Best Restaurant Guide, or *The SBS Eating Guide to Sydney.*

The cost of a three course meal or the equivalent (without drinks) is categorised as follows:
$ = under A$0
$$ = $A20-$50
$$$ = $A50-80
$$$$ = $A80-100

The Finest Restaurants

Buon Ricordo
108 Boundary Street, Paddington
Tel: 9360 6729
Lunch Fri, Sat; dinner Tues–Sat. Licensed. Though the style of cooking is Neapolitan, there are local innovations, such as baked figs with gorgonzola and prosciutto ham, a variation of the traditional Italian dish, prosciutto and melon. A selection of Italian wines is available. $$$

Claudes
10 Oxford Street, Wollahra
Tel: 9331 2353
Dinner Tues–Sat, BYO only
Fixed price $100.
The menu is described as French, but other influences – particularly Asian – have crept in. Try lamb baked with samphire, a salty, succulent plant that grows on tidal flats, with a bottle of Grange. $$$$

left: searching for bargains at Paddington Bazaar
above: a Bronte café

Darley Street Thai
28–30 Bayswater Road, Kings Cross
Tel: 9358 6530
Dinner daily. Fixed price $70 for six courses or à la carte. Licensed.
The menu is so exotic, the waiters explain it before you order. Try the chicken livers stir-fried with smoked fish, prawns, yellow beans and garlic chive flowers. The wine list stresses unwooded, fruit-driven whites – riesling, sauvignon blanc, sémillon – that complement the tangy, spicy flavours of the food. $$$

Rockpool
107 George Street, The Rocks
Tel: 1925 1888
Lunch Mon–Fri; dinner Mon–Sat
Licensed
Sydney's premier seafood restaurant. Try the Chinese pigeon with shiitake mushroom lasagne, which exemplifies Australia's fusion of styles. $$$$

Tetsyuyas
729 Darling Street, Rozelle
Tel: 9555 1017
Lunch Tues–Sat; dinner Tues–Fri.
Licensed and BYO. 6-course dinner $100; 5-course lunch $70.
Tetsuya Wakuda combines French and Japanese cooking techniques with the freshest of Australian seafood and other ingredients to produce Sydney's most exciting food. Try the confit of ocean trout on a bed of briny konbu and sweet leeks. $$$$

Theatrical Settings

Bel Mondo
Level 3, Argyle Department Store 12–14 Argyle Street, The Rocks
Tel: 9241 3700
Lunch Mon–Fri; dinner daily. A la carte. Licensed
The chef presides over the preparation of Italian-style food in an open kitchen on a raised dais. Try the potato gnocchi with truffles, battered zucchini flowers stuffed with gruyere, or braised rabbit with artichokes and potato. The wine list is extensive and exotic. $$$

MG Garage
490 Crown Street, Surry Hills
Tel: 9383 9383
Lunch Mon–Fri; dinner Mon–Sat
Licensed
You can sit at a table next to a shiny MG sports car while you enjoy a salad of snails, pig's trotters, pig's ears and purslane. $$$

Scaling the heights

The Forty One
Level 41, Chifley Tower, 2 Chifley Square
Tel: 9221 2500
Lunch Sun–Fri; dinner Mon–Sat
Licensed
Panoramic views from Manly to Botany Bay, with a solid, middle-of-the-road modern menu and the city's best wine list. $$$$

International
14th floor, 227 Victoria Street, Kings Cross
Tel: 9360 9080
Lunch Fri; dinner daily. Licensed.
Big night out for trendies young and old Slip into a padded booth and sip a Guavarista while admiring the retro-chic décor and panoramic view. Modern Australian menu with wine list to match. Separate menu for vegetarians $$$

The Summit
Level 47, Australia Square, 264 George Street
Tel: 9247 9777
Lunch and dinner daily. Licensed.
Revolving restaurant, decorated in space age style, with cocktail bar, tinkling piano and buffet. $$$

Above: al fresco lunch

Unkai

*Level 36, ANA Hotel, 176 Cumberland
Street, The Rocks*
Tel: 9250 6123
Lunch Sun–Fri; dinner daily, Licensed.
The highest Japanese restaurant in Sydney. Be sure to reserve a window-side
table when booking. $$$

With a view

Beach Road Restaurant

1 Beach Road, Palm Beach
Tel: 9947 11159
Lunch Tues–Sun in summer, Fri–Sun in
winter; dinner daily. BYO.
Impeccable modern Australian food in
a palmy setting. For the quintessential
Sydney dining experience, book a table
for 7pm on a fine summer evening after a day on the beach. Bring bottles of
aged Hunter sémillon and shiraz. $$

Bennelong

Sydney Opera House, Bennelong Point
Tel: 9250 7548
Lunch daily; dinner Mon–Sat. Licensed.
This cathedral-like restaurant in the Opera
House serves modish food on three levels,
all with fine views of Circular Quay. $$$

Boathouse on Blackwattle Bay

End of Ferry Road, Glebe
Tel: 9518 9011
Lunch and dinner Tues–Sun.
Fine fish dishes in a converted boathouse
on a Sydney Harbour backwater. $$$

Doyle's on the Beach

→ THE BEST DOYLES — MUST HAVE LOBSTER

11 Marine Parade, Watsons Bay
Tel: 9337 2001
Lunch and dinner daily. Licensed.
Pricey but good fish and chips with view
down the harbour to the Harbour Bridge.
Take ferry from Circular Quay. $$$

Imperial Peking Afloat

*Cnr Lyne Park & New Southhead Road,
Rose Bay*
Tel: 9371 7955
Lunch and dinner daily. Licensed.
A floating Chinese restaurant with great
views and decent menu. One of the less
expensive waterside dining venues. $$

Right: the ocean view from Jonah's

Jonah's

69 Bynya Road, Palm Beach
Tel: 9974 5599
Breakfast Sat and Sun; lunch, dinner daily.
Licensed
Endless vistas of beaches, islands and
headlands; specialising in Mediterranean
and modern Australian cuisine and also
featuring an excellent wine list. If you want
to extend your peninsula idyll, take advantage of one of Jonah's six adjoining
rooms. $$$

Quay (Bilsons)

*Overseas Passenger Terminal, Circular
Quay West*
Tel: 9252 5600
Lunch Mon–Fri; dinner daily. Licensed.
Highly inspired cuisine with a definite
French influence, in a location just a few
hundred metres across Sydney Cove from
the Opera House. $$$$

An ethnic selection

Abhis

163 Concord Road, North Strathfield
Tel: 9743 3061
Lunch Mon–Fri; dinner daily. BYO
Tucked away in deepest suburbia, this reliable eatery specialises in traditional Indian dishes, particularly those with Goan
influences, using essentially non-Indian
ingredients such as veal and yabbies (small
freshwater crayfish). $$

Asian food halls

Dixon Street, Haymarket, in the basements of the Harbour Plaza and Dixon House, and also on the first floor of the Sussex Centre.

Daily continuous. Licensed.

To sample the range of Asian food available in Sydney, and to eat cheaply and quickly, start here. Each food hall has about a dozen independently leased stalls serving a range of Chinese, Malaysian, Vietnamese, Indonesian and Japanese dishes. The food is either already prepared, or is cooked before you in a few minutes. A basic but sustaining meal for two of short or noodle soup, followed by a choice of Sichuan prawns, Mongolian lamb or roast duck and noodles, together with rice and Chinese vegetables with oyster sauce, will cost about $20.

Arun Thai

28 Macleay Street, Potts Point
Tel: 9357 7414

Lunch and dinner Wed–Mon. Licensed.
The unusual décor – in the style of an 18th-century Thai nobleman's house – supports the quiet and relaxed atmosphere, and complements the traditional Thai food. The stunning wine list would grace the very best European or modern-Australian restaurants. $$

Bay Tinh

318 Victoria Road, Marrickville
Tel: 9560 8673

Dinner daily. BYO
The owner was formerly chef to the prime minister of Vietnam. In this incarnation, he offers an excellent and amazingly inexpensive introduction to Vietnamese food, Sydney-style. $$

BBQ King

18-20 Goulburn Street, Haymarket
Tel: 9264 3741

Lunch and dinner daily
Some of Sydney's most authentic roasted duck, barbecued pork, noodles and steamed vegetables served in an atmosphere redolent of imperial Canton. $$

Casa Asturiana

77 Liverpool Street, City
Tel: 9264 1010.

Lunch Fri and Sun; dinner daily. Tapas bar, Tues–Sat
Licensed and BYO
This restaurant is one of the main reasons why Sydney's Little Spain enjoys the reputation it does today. Begin with a selection of tapas and a glass of *fino* sherry, followed by the best seafood paella for two outside of Barcelona, and a refreshing glass of rosé wine. $$

Above: serving yam cha at Kam Fok – Sydney's largest Chinese restaurant

Dhaba House
466 Cleveland Street, Surry Hills
Tel: 9319 6260
Wed–Sun; dinner daily. BYO
Formerly a laundromat on the bustling Cleveland Street, Dhaba House retains a noisy atmosphere, redolent of downtown Calcutta. Serves no-frills Indian food as authentic as you can get in Sydney at astoundingly low prices. $

El Manara
143 Haldon Street, Lakemba
Tel: 9740 6762
Lunch, dinner daily. No alcohol allowed. Extremely cheap and authentic Lebanese food. $

Elio
159 Norton Street, Leichhardt
Tel: 9560 9129
Lunch Sun; dinner daily
Licensed and BYO
Moderately priced modern Italian cuisine (ie: not big on traditional dishes of the spaghetti bolognese variety) in the heart of Little Italy. $$

Fish Markets Sushi Bar
Blackwattle Bay, Pyrmont
Tel: 9552 2872
Breakfast, lunch daily. BYO
Japanese seafood in one of the world's great fish markets. $

Gaucho Grill
164 Parramatta Road, Stanmore
Tel: 9519 6019.
Lunch Mon–Fri; dinner Mon–Sat
Licensed and BYO
Seafood and meats barbecued as they do it down Argentine way. If you're feeling particularly peckish, order a monster king fillet steak topped with grilled prawn and pepper sauce. $$

Golden Century
393–399 Sussex Street, Haymarket
Tel: 9212 3901
Lunch, dinner daily. Licensed
Chinese-style seafood at its best, and with all the hustle and bustle of Hong Kong before it was returned to China. $$

Kam Fok
Level 3, Market City, 9–13 Hay Street, Haymarket
Tel: 9211 8988
Lunch, dinner daily. Licensed
Sydney's biggest Chinese restaurant and *yum cha* (dumplings) venue. Go for brunch on Sunday and watch the waiters communicate by walkie-talkie as they serve some 800 patrons with a traditional Chinese breakfast. $$

Machiavelli
123 Clarence Street, Sydney
Tel: 9299 3748
Lunch, dinner Mon–Fri. Licensed
This big, loud Italian restaurant is a favourite haunt of many of Sydney's power brokers. The massive antipasto dishes are the city's best. $$$

Oh Calcutta
251 Victoria Street, Darlinghurst
Tel: 9360 3650
Lunch Fri; dinner daily. BYO
One of Sydney's best and most popular Indian restaurants has come up with an eclectic menu by fusing north and south Indian techniques with those of Pakistan and Afghanistan, and using the best Australian produce. $$

Sailor's Thai Canteen
106 George Street, The Rocks
Tel: 9251 2466
Lunch, dinner daily. Licensed
Cheap modern Thai in historic Rocks. A more up-market version downstairs. $$$

Steki Taverna
2 O'Connell Street, Newtown
Tel: 9516 2191
Dinner Wed–Sun. Licensed
Traditional Greek fare just off busy King Street. Live entertainment and dancing at weekends. $$

Unas
338–340 Victoria Street, Darlinghurst
Tel: 9360 6885
Breakfast, lunch, dinner daily. BYO
A Kings Cross perennial specialising in hearty German/Austrian food. $

eating out

NIGHTLIFE

In some of the city's clubs and rock pubs you will be uncomfortable if you are over 30; in others if you are under 30. Singles (both gay and straight) and couples are welcome at most of the following nightspots. Single women are pestered no more than in comparable cities.

Dress codes vary, from *de rigueur* designer fashion to 'neat casual'. Sloppy or dirty clothing will often keep you out on the street. If you are one of those who look eternally young, you must have ID to prove that you're over 18 (the minimum legal drinking age). For up-to-date listings, consult Friday's *Sydney Morning Herald* Metro entertainment supplement. Check out the website: www.sydney.citysearch.com.au for an updated entertainment guide.

Jazz

As is the case in all major Western cities, the jazz scene is in constant flux. Happily, quite a few places in Sydney have survived the shifts of fad and fashion.

The Basement
29 Reiby Place, Circular Quay
Tel: 9251 2797
One of Sydney's best venues, often featuring international acts in addition to various local bands.

Soup Plus
383 George Street, City
Tel: 9299 7728
Basement restaurant presenting an array of styles including trad, mainstream and occasional bop groups.

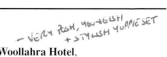
— VERY POSH, YOUNGISH + STYLISH YUPPIE SET

Woollahra Hotel,
Cnr Queen & Moncur Streets
Woollahra
Tel: 9363 2782
Accomplished contemporary groups on Sunday evenings. Well-heeled vibe.

Rock and Pop

Not like it was in local rock's heyday of the late 1970s and early 1980s, but still a good, varied and vibrant scene.

Annandale Hotel
17 Parramatta Road, Annandale
Tel: 9550 1078
Just on the edge of the inner western suburbs, this long-running venue is a great place for acoustic music.

Selina's
Coogee Bay Hotel, cnr Coogee Bay Road & Arden Street, Coogee
Tel: 9665 000
Suburban venue that attracts big names.

The Metro
624 George Street, City
Tel: 9264 2666
Sydney's main rock venue, this is, in terms of visibility and other such customer comforts, the best place to hear and *see* live music. Features international and local acts.

Folk & Blues

Folk and blues are increasingly popular in Sydney, particularly among those in their thirties, but also with twenty-somethings bored with rock and pop.

The Cat & Fiddle Hotel
456 Darling Street, Balmain
Tel: 9810 7931
Mainly acoustic pop, folk and blues.

Harbourside Brasserie
Pier1, Hickson Road, Walsh Bay
Tel: 9252 3000
Blues, world music, jazz, funk, comedy.

Round Midnight
2 Roslyn Street, Kings Cross
Tel: 9356 4045
Mostly R&B, with a bit of jazz, at the heart of Sydney's late-night district.

Bars and Nightclubs
See for yourself whether Sydney has after-dark street cred. Take lots of cash and, in some cases, wear smart clothes.

Grand Pacific Blue Room
Oxford Street, Paddington
Tel: 9331 7108
One of the hottest, hippest nightspots.

Horizons Bar
ANA Hotel, 176 Cumberland Street, The Rocks
Tel: 9250 6000
Sensational views and sophisticated air, but watch the tab – it gets big quick.

Krug Room,
Restaurant Forty One, Level 41, Chifley Tower, 2 Chifley Square, City
Tel: 9221 2500
Luxury drinking with views stretching from the Blue Mountains to the Pacific. Prices start at around $15 per glass.

Slip Inn
11 Sussex Street, City
Tel: 9299 4777
Young merchant bankers mix easily with arty types.

The Soho Lounge
171 Victoria Street, Kings Cross
Tel: 9358 6511
Great pub atmosphere, good prices and mixed crowd, including some of the city's more sophisticated citizens.

Traditional Pubs
Sydney has plenty of renovated, old-style pubs. These places are friendly, inexpensive and many serve food.

Customs House Bar
Sydney Renaissance Hotel, Macquarie Place, City
Tel: 9259 7316
Down near the quay, this is a great place on a Friday afternoon when the after-work crowd flows out to the pavement.

Hero of Waterloo
81 Lower Fort, Millers Point
Tel: 9252 4553
The emphasis is on heritage in this, one of Sydney's oldest pubs.

Lord Nelson Brewery Hotel
19 Kent Street, The Rocks
Tel: 9251 4044
Charming historic atmosphere in Sydney's oldest neighbourhood.

Royal Hotel
Five Ways, Paddington
Tel: 9331 2604
Ornate Victorian architecture with deep verandas and good food and wine.

Watsons Bay (Doyles) Hotel
1 Military Road, Watsons Bay
Tel: 9337 4299
The best location for a long, slow drink on a sunny afternoon, this old pub, with its beer garden and foreshore setting, is a Sydney institution. Catch the ferry from Circular Quay.

Gay
There is no shortage of gay venues in Sydney, with the majority based around Oxford Street. Check out *The Sydney Star Observer*, which provides a comprehensive listing.

Albury Hotel
6 Oxford Street, Paddington
Tel: 9361 6555
This is the place for a quiet, relaxing drink during the week, though business picks up at weekends.

eft: drinking in Darlinghurst

DMC Nightclub
33 Oxford Street, Darlinghurst
Tel: 9267 7380
Renowned gay venue.

Gilligans
Oxford Hotel, Darlinghurst
Tel: 9331 3467
Gay cocktail bar.

Midnight Shift
85 Oxford Street, Darlinghurst
Tel: 9360 4319
Famous, long-running gay nightclub popular with those who like extremes.

Casino

Star City Casino
355 Bulwara Road, Ultimo
Tel: 9777 9000 or 1800 700700 (toll-free).
Located in Darling Harbour, the casino has acres of tables set within areas designed to look like the Australian landscape. Also shops, cafés, bars, discos, live shows and a 352-room hotel.

Coffee Stops

Coffee shops come in clusters. The best place for that morning heart-starter is along Victoria Street in Kings Cross, between William Street (look for the fire station) and Burton Street. Try **Coluzzi** (tel: 9380 5420), the **Tropicana** (tel: 9360 9809) or **Parmalat** (tel: 9331 2914). On the other side of the Cross, there are some great places around Macleay Street; the best is **La Buvette** (65 Macleay Street, entrance off Challis Avenue; tel: 9358 5113). Other in-

ner-city spots good for coffee and an imaginative snack/meal include King Street in Newtown, Glebe Point Road in Glebe and Oxford Street, Paddington. Stanley Street in east Sydney (between Crown and Riley streets) is a reliable little pocket, with the best bet being the long-running **Bill and Toni's** (tel: 9360 4702). The cafés along the beachfront at Bronte are great, but **Bondi Beach** is the surf coast's star café location. Try **Gusto** (16 Hall Street; tel: 9130 4565) or **Sports Bard** (32 Campbell Parade; tel: 9130 4582).

Performing Arts

Theatre, concerts, ballet and opera thrive in Sydney. The big performance venues are the Sydney Opera House (tel: 9250 7111), the Capitol Theatre (tel: 9320 5000), the Theatre Royal (tel: 9320 9191), the sumptuous State Theatre (tel: 9320 9050), Her Majesty's (tel: 9212 3411) and the wonderfully located Wharf Theatre (tel: 9250 1777), where sensational harbour views have made many an audience member return late after the interval. Check out Metro, the entertainment guide in *The Sydney Morning Herald* on Fridays. Tickets for performances are available at the venues or through a ticket agency. You can buy half-price tickets for a number of shows, but only over the counter on the day of the performance, at Half-Tix, 201 Sussex Street (Mon–Fri, 9am–5pm, Sat 10am–3pm).

Movies

Most of the big cinemas are in George Street (between Bathurst and Liverpool streets), where Hollywood releases are screened. See the Friday Metro section in *The Sydney Morning Herald* for listings. Cinemas showing arty and foreign language films include the **Academy Twin** (3a Oxford Street, Paddington) **The Verona** (17 Oxford Street, Paddington; tel: 936 6099) and the **The Dendy** (19 Martin Place; tel: 9233 8166). Check out the **Panasonic Imax** (Southern Promenade, Darling Harbour; tel: 928 3300) for adventure and kids' films specially made for this format.

Above: the Opera House comes alive at night

CALENDAR OF EVENTS

Transport and hotel bookings are very heavy during the school holidays, so book well in advance. Approximate times for school vacations are:

Christmas/Summer: end of December to end of January.
Autumn: early to mid-April.
Winter: early to mid-July.
Spring: late September to early October.

January–May

26 January: Australia Day. Celebrates the arrival of the First Fleet in 1788. Public holiday, speeches, fireworks, etc.

January: Concerts in The Domain. Free performance at night by Opera Australia and the Sydney Symphony Orchestra.

January: Sydney Festival. A month-long programme of local and imported music and theatre (tel: 8248 6500).

Late February/early March: Gay and Lesbian Mardi Gras. One of the biggest parades of its kind in the world, plus a huge dance party, all preceded by a season of gay art and theatre (tel: 9557 4332).

March: Golden Slipper Festival. Popular horse-racing event (tel: 9930 4000).

March/April: RAS Easter Show. The country comes to town; rodeos, wood-chopping, cattle contests, sideshows (tel: 9704 1111).

March: Archibald, Wynne and Sulman exhibitions. Sydney's most popular art event (tel: 9225 1700).

April: Sydney International Dragon Boat Festival (tel: 9525 2893).

May: Sydney Writers' Festival. Book-readings, public lectures and special literary events (tel: 9566 4158).

May/June: National Rugby League State of Origin Series (tel: 9339 8500).

June–December

June: Sydney Film Festival (tel: 9660 3844).

July (even-numbered years): Sydney Biennial. International arts festival, featuring the best works in the contemporary scene (tel: 9368 1411).

August: (first Sunday) City-to-Surf Race. Thousands of runners race from the city to Bondi (tel: 9282 2747).

September: Rugby League, Rugby Union and Australian Football League Grand Finals.

September: Royal Botanic Gardens Spring Festival. Spectacular seasonal displays, complete with brass bands, art shows and food stalls (tel: 9237 8111).

September: Spring Racing Carnival. Sydney's top racing event culminating in the Sydney Cup (tel: 9663 8400).

September/October: Aurora New World Festival. A multicultural celebration at Darling Harbour (tel: 9286 0111).

October: Manly Jazz Festival. Musicians from around the world come together to jam (tel: 9977 1088).

December: Carols in The Domain. Sydney's favourite music event.

26 December: Start of Sydney-to-Hobart Yacht Race.

31 December: Public holiday, special events and fireworks to mark New Year's Eve.

Above: celebrating in Chinatown

Practical Information

GETTING THERE

By Air

Sydney is Australia's major international gateway, serviced by flights from Asia, the Pacific, Europe, Africa and North America. Some 30 international airlines have regular scheduled flights to Sydney. The city is also well served by daily domestic flights. Sydney (Kingsford Smith) Airport is on Botany Bay, 9km (5½ miles) from the city centre. The three terminals are: the international at the western side of the airport, and the two adjacent domestic terminals of Qantas and Ansett Australia.

Government buses operate regularly between the international and domestic terminals. Alternatively, take a taxi, though this option will cost you more. Both can be found at the entrance to any terminal. There is no rail link yet between the airport and the city, but one was due to open in 2000. From all airport terminals take the yellow Airport Express bus (No 300 to the city and No 350 to Kings Cross; tel: 131500), which takes about 30 minutes to reach the city and a similar time to Kings Cross. Both buses go via Central Railway Station. A taxi is faster but will cost about A$20.

Sydney's narrow roads get very crowded during peak-hour traffic. If you are departing from Sydney during the afternoon rush, allow up to an hour to get to the airport.

All the main rental-car companies (Avis, Hertz, Budget, Thrifty etc) have outlets at each of the terminals. New South Wales Tourism operates an information centre in the arrival hall of the international terminal. This can supply you with information and maps of Sydney, and also assist you in booking accommodation (tel: 9667 9111).

By Rail

The terminal for all rail journeys into Sydney is Central Railway (known simply as 'Central') at the southern end of the city centre.

Left: Harbour regatta
Right: arriving in style

Unfortunately there are virtually no hotels in walking range (particularly if you are carrying heavy baggage) of Central Railway.

There is an adjoining electric-train station with regular services to the city centre and the suburbs, but to get to it you'll have to negotiate some flights of steps. A taxi from Central Railway to downtown or to a Kings Cross hotel will cost about A$8. Alternatively, there is a bus stop with regular departures to the city and the suburbs.

By Bus

There is an extensive inter-state bus system and fares are cheaper than rail or air prices. Most bus terminals are on the fringes of the city centre. You'll probably need a government city bus or taxi to get to your hotel.

TRAVEL ESSENTIALS

When to Visit

Any time is fine, though obviously summer (Dec–Feb) is hotter, and winter (June–Aug) is colder and windier. The seasons are the opposite of those found in the Northern Hemisphere. Spring (Sept–Nov) and autumn (Mar–May) are delightful times, usually with clear blue skies.

Visas and Passports

All visitors require a passport and visa to enter Australia, except New Zealanders, who need a passport only. Visas are free and valid for up to six months. In some cases applications must be made to the nearest Australian or British government representative, but the introduction of electronic-transfer authority (ETA) visas has enabled travel agents to handle most requests on the spot. An onward or return ticket, and sufficient funds, are required.

To extend your stay, contact the Department of Immigration (head office: 477 Pitt Street, Sydney; tel: 131881) a month before your visa expires. You will have to show sufficient funds and an onward ticket. The maximum time, including extensions, allowed to visitors is a year.

Vaccinations

Vaccinations are not required if you are flying directly to Australia and have not been to areas infected by smallpox, yellow fever, cholera or typhoid in the 14 days prior to your arrival.

Customs

Visitors aged 18 and over are allowed to bring in 250gm of cigarette products, 1.125 litres of alcohol and other dutiable goods to the value of A$400, plus personal clothing, footwear and toiletries. Children under the age of 18 are allowed A$200 worth of dutiable goods in their personal baggage. An extra bottle of alcohol is permitted if goods are under A$400 in value.

Australia has very strict regulations on the importation of foods, plants, animals and their by-products. Almost anything of this nature will be confiscated at Customs. Australia is rabies-free and all incoming animals are placed in quarantine. The minimum period for cats and dogs – including guide dogs – is six months. For further information call the Customs Information Centre (tel 1300 363 263, or 612 6275 6666 if you're not in Australia). Drug smuggling of *any* kind results in long jail sentences.

Weather

March and June are the wettest months, July the coldest, January and February the hottest. Mean temperatures are: summer 21.7°C (71°F); autumn 18.1°C (64.6°F); winter 12.6°C (54.7°F); spring 17.4°C (63.3°F).

Clothing

For a summer visit, bring a sweater or jacket (for the occasional cool spell), an umbrella, swimming costume, sunglasses, sunhat and a pair of good walking shoes. In spring

Above: Sydneysiders on Bondi's promenade

and autumn, have light- to medium-weight clothes. For winter, pack warm clothes, a raincoat and umbrella. Though it never snows in Sydney, and the temperature rarely gets below about 10°C (50°F), the weather can get chilly. Australians tend to dress casually; lightweight, comfortable clothes are ideal for Sydney. For dining at the better hotels and restaurants, a jacket and tie may be required.

Electricity
The current is 240/250 volts, 50 hertz. Most good hotels and motels have universal outlets for 110-volt shavers and small appliances. For larger appliances such as hairdryers, you will need a converter and flat three-pin adaptor.

Time Differences
Australian Eastern Standard Time is 10 hours ahead of Greenwich Mean Time, 30 minutes ahead of Adelaide and Darwin, and two hours ahead of Perth. Daylight saving time is between October and March.

GETTING ACQUAINTED

Geography
On the southeast coast of New South Wales, Sydney spreads over 1,736 sq km (670 sq miles), and is much bigger than Rome or Los Angeles County. The population density is a low 277 people per sq km. Straddled by Sydney Harbour Bridge, the harbour bisects north and south Sydney; the city centre is on the southern shore. The western suburbs, spreading to the foothills of the Blue Mountains, are the most populous area.

Government & Economy
New South Wales's two-chamber parliament is elected every four years – voting is mandatory for adults over 18. The federal government legislates from Canberra, and there is a third tier of local municipal councils.

New South Wales has a healthy mixed economy of primary industries (coal, wheat, wool, dairy, wine etc), secondary (steelmaking, manufacturing etc) and tertiary industries. Education, the arts, banking and insurance are major players in the state economy. Almost half of Australia's 100 biggest corporations have headquarters in Sydney.

Nearly 3 million tourists from all over the world visit the city each year.

Population
As Australia's largest, oldest and liveliest city, with a population of almost 4 million, Sydney represents a very diverse mixture of nations, tongues, creeds and colours. Almost one-third of its people were born overseas, and the city continues to attract some 40 percent of the nation's new immigrants each year. Earlier waves of settlers from the British Isles were supplemented by large numbers of post-World War II migrants from northern and southern Europe. Since the 1970s, there have been increasing numbers of Middle Eastern and Asian settlers, especially from Lebanon, Vietnam, China and Hong Kong.

MONEY MATTERS

Currency
The currency is the Australian dollar. Coins come in 5-, 10-, 20- and 50-cent, $1 and $2 denominations. Notes are $5, $10, $50 and $100. You may bring in or take out a maximum of A$10,000 (or its equivalent in foreign currency) in cash. Larger amounts must be declared. As of July 2000, all goods and services (fresh food excluded) are subject to a 10 percent tax at the point of purchase.

Foreign Exchange
Most foreign currencies can be exchanged at the airport. City banks change money between 9.30am and 5pm on weekdays. International-class hotels will change major currencies for guests. There are bureaux de change in major tourist areas, but elsewhere they are few and far between, so change your foreign currency before venturing out.

Credit Cards
The most widely accepted cards are American Express, Diners Club, Mastercard and Visa. Small establishments might not take lesser-known cards. If you have a card-related problem, call one of the following:
American Express: 1800-804 874
Diners Club: 1300-360 060
MasterCard: 1800-120 113
Visa: 1800-805 341

Travellers' Cheques

All well-known international travellers' cheques can be cashed at airports, banks, hotels, motels and the like. There are Thomas Cook and American Express offices in the city centre. Encashment fees and rates of exchange vary. For lost travellers cheques call:
American Express: 1800 251 902
Thomas Cook: 1800 127 495

Tipping

Tipping is not obligatory but a small gratuity for good service is appreciated. Hairdressers and taxi drivers don't expect tips. In restaurants, it is customary to tip waiters up to 10 percent of the bill for good service.

Departure Tax

A departure tax of A$30 is payable by all travellers, but is nearly always included in the ticket price of international airfares.

GETTING AROUND

Taxis

You can hire a cab wherever you see one vacant. The flagdown fee is A$2; thereafter, A$1.17 per km travelled. Phone bookings cost A$1 extra. Smoking isn't permitted in public vehicles, so ask your driver before you light up. Be sure the driver knows the way if you're going to an obscure place. If you have a complaint, call the taxi firm with the driver's – and his cab's – number (every driver must display a photo and ID card). Taxi companies serving the inner city are:
Premier Cabs, tel: 9637 9322
Taxis Combined Services, tel: 9020 2000
Legion Cabs, tel: 131451
Water-taxi firms serving the harbour are:
Aqua Cabs, tel: 9922 4252
Taxis Afloat, tel: 9955 3222

Urban Trains, Buses and Ferries

The State Transit Authority publishes a free map of Sydney's train, bus and ferry services, available from the State Transit Authority Travel & Tours Centre (11–13 York Street); information kiosks at Circular Quay, Wynyard Square and the Queen Victoria Building, which has free timetables.

Trains

Sydney has an extensive electric train service – by far the quickest way to get around. Trains run frequently, and all services connect at the City Circle underground system.

Buses

Extensive bus services are run mostly by the State Transit Authority, with the main terminals located at Circular Quay, Wynyard Square and at the Central Railway Station.

Sydney Explorer red buses roam through a 20-km (12½-mile) circuit of Sydney's city sights, and will let you off at any of 24 stops with the option to rejoin the bus later. Tickets cost A$28 for adults, A$20 for children and A$75 for families. The Sydney Explorer leaves at 17-minute intervals from Circular Quay, from 8.40am to 6.50pm daily. The round trip takes about 90 minutes. Purchase tickets on board the bus.

Alternatively, there is a blue Bondi and Bay Explorer bus service that covers a 35-km (22-mile) circuit of the eastern suburbs, including Double Bay and Watsons Bay, and across to Bondi Beach, daily from 9.15am to 5.55pm. Fares are as per the Sydney Explorer. The Olympic Explorer, the latest tourist route, tours Homebush Bay. Catch a train from the city, and join the bus at the station.

The Sydney pass gives you unlimited rides on the train, ferry and bus (including the Explorer and Tramway). It also covers the Sydney Ferries cruises, including the Harbour Cruise, River Cruise and Harbour Lights Cruise. The Sydney pass costs $85 for 3 days, $115 for 5 days and $135 for 7 days. For transport information call the Infoline (tel: 131500) between 6am and 10pm daily.

Ferries and Cruises

Ferries are the nicest way of getting around Sydney. They depart from Circular Quay where the State Transit Authority issues free

Left: vintage car in a modern city

timetables. The longest regular ferry runs are to Parramatta and Manly; the former takes 1 hour, 10 minutes, the latter takes 35 minutes. The 10-minute ride to Kirribilli offers a panorama of the city skyline.

Ferry services are also available from the Royal National Park to the south (Cornulla National Park Ferry Cruises, tel: 9523 2990) and Pittwater to the north (Palm Beach Ferry Service, tel: 9974 5235). There are a variety of commercial harbour cruises, and lunchtime and supper cruises such as Captain Cook Harbour Cruises, from Circular Quay wharf No 6 and the Aquarium Wharf of Darling Harbour. Departing morning, afternoon and night, the cruises include commentary, coffee, lunch or dinner.

Monorail and Light Rail

A monorail runs between Darling Harbour and the city. The fare is A\$2.80, or A\$6 a day, and trains run every five minutes, Mon–Sat, 7am–10pm, Sun 8am–10pm.

The Sydney Light Rail runs between Central Station and Pyrmont every five minutes. For both services tel: 9552 2288.

HOURS & HOLIDAYS

Business Hours

Retail hours are generally, Mon–Fri 9am–5.30pm, Sat 9am–4pm. Thursday night features shopping until 9pm. Restaurants, snack bars, bookshops and local corner stores are open till late in the evening and sometimes all weekend. Banks are open Mon–Thurs 9.30am–4pm, and Fri till 5pm.

Public Holidays

Banks, post offices, offices and most shops close on the following public holidays:

New Year's Day 1 January
Australia Day 26 January
ANZAC Day 25 April
Good Friday (3 days) April/May
Queen's Birthday 2nd Monday in June
Bank Holiday 1st Monday in August
Labour Day 1st Monday in October
Christmas Day 25 December
Boxing Day 26 December
New Year's Eve 31 December

ACCOMMODATION

Sydney's many hotels range from top-class to the unsalubrious. Tourist information offices have details of accommodation options, and bookings can be made at any travel agent. Popular locations include the city, The Rocks, Darling Harbour, Kings Cross and Bondi Beach. The Travellers Information Services at Eddy Avenue, Central Railway Station (daily 6am–10.30pm; tel: 9669 5111) can assist with standby accommodation at 3, 4 and 5-star hotels; and it accepts overseas bookings. The flat 10 percent tax on all accommodation in New South Wales might change with the introduction of a general goods and services tax in July 2000.

Above: one of the finest views in the world

Deluxe

A well-appointed room in a luxury hotel can cost from A$230 to about A$450 (single or double) – but better deals are available if you shop around. Air-conditioning, private bathrooms, TV, king-size beds and minibars are standard in all of these lavish establishments. Most opened in the past few years.

ANA Hotel
176 Cumberland Street, The Rocks, Sydney 2000
Tel: 9250 6000
Fax: 9250 6250
E-mail: businesscentre@anahotel.com.au
A grand hotel that opened in 1992, this All Nippon Airways' establishment has wonderful views of Harbour Bridge and across Sydney Cove to the Opera House. A class act that's hard to beat.

Hotel Inter-Continental
117 Macquarie Street, Sydney 2000
Tel: 9230 0200
Fax: 9240 1240
E-mail: sydney@interconti.com
Soaring out of the shell of the historic Treasury building in the business district, this 31-storey, 498-room hotel combines old-world style and modern facilities.

Manly Pacific Parkroyal
55 North Steyne, Manly 2095
Tel: 9977 7666
Fax: 9977 7822
E-mail: admin@manly.parkroyal.com.au
Situated right on Manly Beach, the 170-room Manly Pacific is 30 minutes from the city by ferry and retains the relaxed character of a seaside resort.

Sydney Marriott
36 College Street, Sydney 2000
Tel: 9361 8400
Fax: 9361 8599
E-mail: reservationsydneymarriott@mirvachotels.com.au
Facing Hyde Park, this 241-room hotel enjoys a fine reputation for the quality of its rooms and service.

Observatory Hotel
89–113 Kent Street, Sydney 2000
Tel: 9256 2222
Fax: 9256 2233
E-mail: observatory@mail.com
The country's first Orient Express Hotel, the 100-room Observatory, which opened in February 1992, is one of the finest of Sydney's luxury hotels. In keeping with its pedigree, it is the last word in service, luxury and facilities.

Park Hyatt Sydney
7 Hickson Road, The Rocks, Sydney 2000
Tel: 9241 1234
Fax: 9256 1555
E-mail: sydney@hyatt.com.au
The Park Hyatt enjoys a perfect location on Sydney Cove. Although there are 158 rooms on four storeys, vacancies are few and far between throughout the year on account of the hotel's incredible views.

Quay West Sydney
98 Gloucester Street, Sydney 2000
Tel: 9240 6000
Fax: 9240 6060
Sandwiched between the Regent and the ANA, the Quay West has, like those hotels, some grand vistas. It boasts 132 spacious apartments with complete kitchens and luxurious fittings. Facilities include sauna, indoor pool and gym.

Regent Sydney
199 George Street, Sydney 2000
Tel: 9238 0000
Fax: 9251 2851
The Regent has enjoyed a reputation as Sydney's finest hotel for most of the past decade. It has a good location at Circular Quay and an impressive atrium foyer. There are 620 rooms on 34 floors.

Above: ANA Hotel

Ritz-Carlton Sydney

93 Macquarie Street, Sydney 2000
Tel: 9252 4600
Fax: 9247 8672
E-mail: reservation@rcsyd.zip.com.au
Grand in the classical American style with antique furniture and welcoming open fires. There are 106 rooms on 10 floors.

The Landmark, Parkroyal

81 Macleay Street, Potts Point 2011
Tel: 9368 3000
Fax: 9357 7600
E-mail: hotel@landmark.parkroyal.com.au
Modern 472-room hotel with fine restaurant. Westward-facing rooms have probably the best views of the city skyline. The area is calmer than adjoining Kings Cross.

The Renaissance Sydney Hotel

30 Pitt Street, Sydney 2000
Tel: 9259 7000
Fax: 9251 1122
This flagship property of the Ramada group in the South Pacific, it opened in the business heart of Sydney in 1989. There are 579 rooms on 32 storeys, but three floors are reserved for Ramada executive club guests.

Expensive

Priced between A$150 and A$230 per room (double or single), these are either three- or four-star hotels. All are well-equipped, with direct-dial telephones, air conditioning, TV/radio and en-suite bathrooms.

Chateau Sydney

14 Macleay Street, Potts Point 2011
Tel: 9358 2500
Fax: 9358 1959
In the centre of Potts Point, this hotel has 96 rooms, a heated pool, barbecue and laundry.

Parkroyal at Darling Harbour

150 Day Street, Sydney 2000
Tel: 9261 4444
Fax: 9261 8766
E-mail:
hotel@darlinghbr.parkroyal.com.au
Opened in 1991 and overlooking Darling Harbour, this 11-storey, 349-room hotel takes full advantage of this recently developed part of town. Just a short walk to the city.

Ravesis on Bondi Beach

Corner of Campbell Parade and Hall Street, Bondi Beach
Tel: 9365 4422
Fax: 9365 1481
Pleasant, boutique-sized hotel with fabulous beach views. Lively street scene.

Regents Court

18 Springfield Avenue, Potts Point 2011
Tel: 9358 1533
Fax: 9358 1833
E-mail: regcourt@iname.com
Sydney's most stylish small hotel, in Kings Cross, attracts an international arts crowd. Features fully equipped kitchens.

Sebel of Sydney

23 Elizabeth Bay Road, Elizabeth Bay
Tel: 9358 3244
Fax: 9357 1926
E-mail: reservationsebelsydney@mirva-chotels.com.au
Quiet, luxurious, intimate centrally located hotel. Popular with celebrities, its facilities include heated pool, gym and sauna.

Moderate

Clean, comfortable hotels from A$80 to A$150 per room (double or single).

Aarons Hotel

37 Vitimo Road, Haymarket
Tel: 9281 5555
Fax: 9281 2666
Good standard motel-style accommodation near Darling Harbour. 94 rooms.

Park Regis

Corner of Castlereagh and Park streets, Sydney 2000
Tel: 9267 6511
Fax: 9264 2252
E-mail: parksyd@maxi.net.au
120 air-conditioned rooms set in the centre of the shopping district, near the town hall.

The Russell

143A George Street, Sydney 2000
Tel: 9241 3543
Fax: 9252 1652
29 rooms, two storeys, in The Rocks area.

Right: at your service

Hostels

The Youth Hostel Association runs two city hostels. The one at 262–264 Glebe Point Road (tel: 9692 8418) has 150 beds in 110 dormitories. Sydney Central YHA (tel: 9281 9111), at the corner of Rawson and Pitt streets opposite Central Railway Station, is reputedly the world's largest hostel, with 545 beds. Facilities include a pool, TV room, large self-catering kitchen, and laundry. The YHA hostel (tel: 9999 2196) off Church Point on Pittwater provides a chance to experience the bush, sun and saltwater lifestyle. A good starting point is VIP Backpacker Resorts of Australia (tel: 07 3268 533), which runs 19 outfits in Sydney.

There are lots of hostels in the Kings Cross area, particularly in Victoria Street. The 186-bed Original Backpackers Hostel, 160–162 Victoria Street, Kings Cross (tel: 9356 3232) is well-run and good value. It offers free pick-ups from the airport and railway stations, e-mail facilities and help in finding employment.

Budget hotels are located mainly in the city, Kings Cross or Bondi areas. There is a 100-bed YWCA (tel: 9264 2451) in the heart of Sydney at 5 Wentworth Avenue, Darlinghurst. In the city, the CB Private Hotel, 417 Pitt Street (tel: 9211 5115) has 200 rooms; directly behind it, the George Street Private Hotel has 57 clean rooms. The Lord Nelson Brewery Hotel (19 Kent Street, The Rocks; tel: 9251 4044) provides cheap, clean and comfortable digs in one of the country's oldest pubs.

HEALTH & EMERGENCIES

Useful Numbers

In an emergency requiring police assistance or ambulance service, or in the case of fire, dial 000. Other emergency numbers: Lifeline (counselling), tel: 131144; Women's Info Service, tel: 1800-817 227; Translation and Intepreting Service, tel: 131450.

Security and Crime

Sydney is a relatively safe city, and you should not worry unduly about being a victim of mugging or theft. But avoid dark lanes at night, lock your hotel room and keep valuables hidden.

Medical

Hospitals and doctors are readily available, but overseas visitors are not covered by the government's Medicare policy. A visit to the doctor will cost A$35 and up. Passport holders from Britain, New Zealand, Ireland, Finland, Italy, the Netherlands, Sweden and Malta are eligible for free basic emergency care at public hospitals, via reciprocal agreements. Buy a travellers' health and accident insurance policy before you leave home.

Pharmacies

Chemists, otherwise known as pharmacies, employ qualified professionals who dispense prescribed medicines. They also carry familiar brands of general medications, cosmetics, toiletries, etc. Visitors are allowed to bring up to four weeks' supply of prescribed drugs. For larger quantities, bring a doctor's certificate to avoid difficulties at Customs. There are a number of late-night pharmacies in the inner city area, mostly around Kings Cross. Ask at your hotel, or ring Chemist Prescriptions after hours (tel: 9235 0333) for information on, and directions to, the nearest pharmacy.

Dental

For dental emergencies, call 9692 0333 or 9692 0598 or, alternatively, consult the Dentists section in the *Yellow Pages*.

Drinking Water

It is safe to drink water straight from the tap in any Australian town. If you prefer bottled mineral water, it's available everywhere.

Sunburn

The summer sun in Sydney is extremely strong. Wear a wide-brimmed hat to protect your face and avoid sunbathing between 10.30am and 3.30pm when the UV rays are strongest. Use a sunscreen with a high Sun Protection Factor.

COMMUNICATIONS

Post

Post offices are open Mon–Fri 9am–5pm. The General Post Office (in Martin Place) is open Mon–Fri 8.15am–5.30pm and Sat

10am–2pm. Post offices will hold mail for visitors, as will American Express offices for AE cardholders. For all postal queries call Australia Post on 131317.

Telephone and Fax

Local calls from public phones cost 40 cents for an unlimited time. STD (Subscriber Trunk Dialling) is for long-distance calls within Australia. STD calls are cheapest between 10pm and 8am.

ISD (International Subscriber Dialling) is used for direct dialling overseas. ISD public phones are fairly common at post offices, airports and hotel foyers. The ISD access code is 0011 followed by the code of the country you are calling. Call 1223 for local-directory assistance; 1225 for overseas assistance; 12552 for information on costs.

Faxes can be sent from international-class hotels or from post offices.

Media

Sydney has two daily newspapers: the broadsheet *Sydney Morning Herald*, and the tabloid *Daily Telegraph*. *The Financial Review* and *The Australian* are national dailies. *The Sydney Morning Herald* is a must on Fridays as it includes the Metro entertainment guide. Sunday is the day for tabloids such as *The Sun-Herald* and *The Sunday Telegraph*.

The weekly magazine *The Bulletin* includes the Australian edition of *Newsweek*. The *Guardian Weekly*, *USA Today* and the *International Herald Tribune* are on sale at most newsagents. Airmail copies of overseas newspapers and journals are available at specialised outlets in Kings Cross or Martin Place.

USEFUL INFORMATION

Tourist Information

The Australian Tourist Commission has 40 offices around the world, but its main point of consumer contact is through its website: www.australia.com. New South Wales Tourism provides detailed information on the Sydney area. Visit its booth on the arrivals level at Sydney International Airport (tel: 9667 9111).

The Travellers Information Service (daily 6am–10.30pm; Eddy Avenue, Central Railway Station; tel: 9669 5111) gives advice on accommodation, tours, shopping, etc. The New South Wales Visitor Information Line (tel: 132077) is good on out-of-town destinations. There are information booths at Circular Quay, Martin Place, Town Hall, Darling Harbour and a number of other places further afield. For perhaps the best range of information, check out the Sydney Visitors Centre (daily 9am–6pm; 106 George Street, The Rocks; tel: 9255 1788).

Sydney for the Disabled

Advance notice with relevant details of your disability will ensure assistance from airlines, hotels and railway offices. Begin at the National Information Communications Network (NICAN), which keeps a database of facilities and services with disabled access. Write to NICAN PO Box 407 Curtain, ACT 2605 (tel: 1800-806 796). Another good point of contact is the State Library of New South Wales Disability Access Service, tel: 9273 1583 (Mon–Fri, 9am–5pm). Specially outfitted taxis can be booked in advance (tel: 1800-043 187).

Gays and Lesbians

Sydney is one of the world's top destinations for gay and lesbian travellers. The city is awash with attractions, and most of the old prejudices are on the way out. Random violence towards gays is not, however, unknown, particularly around the gay heartland of Oxford Street. Avoid trouble by sticking to the main streets, and at night walk with friends. Check *The Sydney Star Observer* for listings. Call the International Gay and Lesbian Travel Association (tel: 9818 669) for details of relevant travel services.

Left: Sydney calling

SPORT

Sailing
Sailing is a popular pastime among Sydneysiders. The yachting season runs Sept–Mar. Races and regattas are held nearly every weekend.

Surf Carnivals
A surf carnival is held at one of Sydney's ocean beaches on most Saturdays, Oct–Mar. The carnivals consist of swimming, board-paddling, surfboating and beach-sprinting events.

Surfboard Riding
In summer and autumn there are surfboard competitions. Listen for the morning radio surf reports on MMM-FM and JJJ-FM.

Yacht Races
Races between 18-footers are held every Saturday. Ferries leave from Milsons Point (tel: 9955 8350) at 2pm. The start of the Sydney-to-Hobart Yacht Race on Boxing Day is a major sporting event in Sydney.

Golf
The New South Wales Golfing Association (tel: 9264 8433) is a good starting point, or check the *Yellow Pages*, then call the course clubhouse for details.

Running and Jogging
Centennial Park, The Domain and Bondi Beach are popular for running or jogging.

Motor Racing
Eastern Creek (tel: 9672 1000) has regular car and motorcycle events all year.

Swimming
Sydney is well equipped with swimming pools. Try Andrew (Bouy) Charlton in The Domain (tel: 9358 6686), Cook and Phillip Park in the city (tel: 9326 0444), or the Bondi Baths (tel: 9130 4804).

Skiing
Expect crowded slopes, fair snow and expensive accommodation during the June–Sept ski season in the Snowy Mountains southwest of Sydney.

Horse Racing
Sydney has six race tracks, of which Randwick is the closest to the city. There are races throughout the year at Canterbury, Rosehill and Warwick Farm. The Sydney Turf Club (tel: 9930 4000) can handle most queries.

Rugby League
Games are played from Mar–Sept at the Sydney Football Stadium, Stadium Australia, and at many suburban venues. Contact the National Rugby League (tel: 9339 8500) for further details.

Cricket
The season runs Oct–Mar with international and interstate matches spread throughout this period. Matches are played at the Sydney Cricket Ground (tel: 9360 6601) and at suburban grounds.

Aerobics
There are no shortage of gyms in the Sydney area, and many have aerobics classes. Try Temple of the Body and Soul in Edgecliff (tel: 9362 9988) or City Gym in East Sydney (tel: 9360 6247).

practical information

Cycling

The Roads and Traffic Authority (tel: 1800-060 607) publishes a map detailing Sydney's extensive bicycle-path network. Call the NSW Cycling Federation (tel: 9796 1344) for details on bike hire and organised tours.

Others

Sydney has lots of tennis courts. Check the *Yellow Pages*. Other sport facilities include hockey pitches, ice- and roller-skating rinks, gliding clubs and squash courts. Enquire at the Sydney Visitors Centre for more details.

FURTHER READING

Travel/General

Best Sydney Bushwalks, by Neil Paton (Kangaroo Press).
A Companion Guide to Sydney, by Ruth Park, revised edition (Duffy & Snelgrove).
Cosmopolitan Sydney: Explore the World in One City, by Jock Collins and Antonio Castillo (Pluto Press).
Insight Guide: Sydney, revised edition 1999 by Ingrid Ohlsson (APA Publications).
Sydney Morning Herald Best of Sydney, edited by Ross Muller (Sydney Morning Herald Books).
The 100 Things Everyone Needs to Know About Sydney, by David Dale (Pan Macmillan).
Walking Sydney, by Lisa Clifford and Mandy Webb (Pan Macmillan).

Food & Wine

Cheap Eats (Universal Magazines).
The Penguin Good Australian Wine Guide, by Mark Shield and Huon Hooke (Penguin).
The SBS Eating Guide, by Maeve O'Mara and Joanna Savill (Allen & Unwin).
The Sydney Morning Herald Good Food Guide, edited by Terry Durack and Jill Dupleix (Anne O'Donovan).

Art & Architecture

Opera House Act One, by David Messent (David Messent Photography).
Sydney Architecture, by Graham Jahn (The Watermark Press).
Sydney: A Guide to Recent Architecture, by Francesca Morrison (Ellipsis London).

Fiction

The Bodysurfers, by Robert Drewe (Pan Macmillan).
Cliff Hardy Series (various titles), by Peter Corris (Allen & Unwin).
For Love Alone and *Seven Poor Men of Sydney*, by Christina Stead (Angus and Robertson).
Foveaux, by Kylie Tennant (Angus and Robertson).
A Harp in the South, by Ruth Park (Penguin).
Illywhacker, by Peter Carey (University of Queensland Press)
Jonah, by Louis Stone (Angus and Robertson).
Poor Man's Orange, by Ruth Park (Penguin).

History & Environment

The Fatal Shore, by Robert Hughes (Collins Harvill).
1788, by Watkin Tench edited and introduced by Tim Flannery (Text).
A Short History of Australia, by C.M.H Clark, (Penguin) and *Manning Clark's History of Australia*, by Manning Clark, abridged by Michael Cathcart (Melbourne University Press)
Sydney, by Geoffrey Moohouse (Allen & Unwin)
Sydney: Biography of a City, by Lucy Hughes (Random House)
Sydney–A Story of a City, by Shirley Fitzgerald (Harper Collins)
The Rocks: Life in Early Sydney, by Grace Karskens (Melbourne University Press).

Biography

A Fence Around the Cuckoo, by Ruth Park (Penguin).
Fishing the Styx, by Ruth Park (Penguin).
Greer: Untamed Shrew, by Christine Wallace (Picador).
Patrick White: A Life, by David Marr (Random House).
Unreliable Memoirs, by Clive James (Picador).

Language & Humour

The Lingo: Listening to Australian English, by Graham Seal (University of New South Wales Press).
The Macquarie Dictionary (Macquarie Library).

Left: 'the finest harbour in the world'

ACKNOWLEDGEMENTS

Photography	**Tony Perrottet** *and*
40	**Marcus Brooke**
11, 12, 23, 24, 25, 38, 49B, 53, 56, 59, 72, 84	**John Borthwick**
10, 13T	**Bridgeman/State Library of NSW**
16	**Jean-Paul Ferrero/Auscape**
15	**FW Flood/ Coo-ee Historical Picture Library**
13B	**Darling Harbour Authority**
54	**Jean-Marc La Roque/Auscape**
22, 60	**David McGonigal**
69	**David Messent**
85	**New South Wales Tourist Board**
14	**State Library of NSW**
68	**Stockshots**
67B	**Stockshots/Roy Bisson**
52	**Stockshots/Geoff Brown**
75	**Stockshots/Phill Castleton**
63, 76	**Stockshots/Myke Gerrish**
50B, 57, 67T	**Stockshots/Graeme Monro**
64, 96	**Stockshots/North Sullivan**
107	**Stockshots/Peter J Robinson**
62	**Stockshots/Clifford White**
Cartography	**Berndtson & Berndtson**
Front and Back Covers	**Tony Perrottet**
Cover Design	**Carlotta Junger**

© APA Publications GmbH & Co. Verlag KG Singapore Branch, Singapore

Left: a backward glance

INSIGHT
Pocket Guides

Insight Pocket Guides pioneered a new approach to guidebooks, introducing the concept of the authors as "local hosts" who would provide readers with personal recommendations, just as they would give honest advice to a friend who came to stay. They also included a full-size pull-out map.

Now, to cope with the needs of the 21st century, new editions in this growing series are being given a new look to make them more practical to use, and restaurant and hotel listings have been greatly expanded.

☼ INSIGHT GUIDE

The world's largest collection visual travel guides

Now in association with

Also from Insight Guides...

Insight Guides is the classic series, providing the complete picture with expert and informative text and stunning photography. Each book is an ideal travel planner, a reliable on-the-spot companion - and a superb visual souvenir of a trip. 193 titles.

Insight Maps are designed to complement the guidebooks. They provide full mapping of major destinations, and their laminated finish gives them ease of use and durability. 85 titles.

Insight Compact Guides are handy reference books, modestly priced yet comprehensive. The text, pictures and maps are all cross-referenced, making them ideal books to consult while seeing the sights. 119 titles.

INSIGHT POCKET GUIDE TITLES

Aegean Islands	California,	Israel	Moscow	Seville, Cordoba &
Algarve	Northern	Istanbul	Munich	Granada
Alsace	Canton	Jakarta	Nepal	Seychelles
Amsterdam	Chiang Mai	Jamaica	New Delhi	Sicily
Athens	Chicago	Kathmandu Bikes	New Orleans	Sikkim
Atlanta	Corsica	& Hikes	New York City	Singapore
Bahamas	Costa Blanca	Kenya	New Zealand	Southeast England
Baja Peninsula	Costa Brava	Kuala Lumpur	Oslo and	Southern Spain
Bali	Costa Rica	Lisbon	Bergen	Sri Lanka
Bali Bird Walks	Crete	Loire Valley	Paris	Sydney
Bangkok	Denmark	London	Penang	Tenerife
Barbados	Fiji Islands	Los Angeles	Perth	Thailand
Barcelona	Florence	Macau	Phuket	Tibet
Bavaria	Florida	Madrid	Prague	Toronto
Beijing	Florida Keys	Malacca	Provence	Tunisia
Berlin	French Riviera	Maldives	Puerto Rico	Turkish Coast
Bermuda	(Côte d'Azur)	Mallorca	Quebec	Tuscany
Bhutan	Gran Canaria	Malta	Rhodes	Venice
Boston	Hawaii	Manila	Rome	Vienna
Brisbane & the	Hong Kong	Marbella	Sabah	Vietnam
Gold Coast	Hungary	Melbourne	St. Petersburg	Yogjakarta
British Columbia	Ibiza	Mexico City	San Francisco	Yucatán Peninsula
Brittany	Ireland	Miami	Sarawak	
Brussels	Ireland's	Montreal	Sardinia	
Budapest	Southwest	Morocco	Scotland	

INDEX

index